THE SEA GIRT HOUSE / DAVID HU ARCHITECT

A HOUSE THAT BREATHES

WITH ITS SURROUNDINGS

MASTERPIECE
SERIES

THE SEA GIRT HOUSE / DAVID HU ARCHITECT

FOREWORD & PROJECT DESCRIPTION BY DAVID HU | INTRODUCTION BY BYRON HAWES |
INTERVIEW BY VLADIMIR BELOGOLOVSKY | PHOTOGRAPHY BY WADE ZIMMERMAN, JAVIER ODDO AND MARK GUMIENNY

OSCAR RIERA OJEDA
PUBLISHERS

CONTENTS

FOREWORD
BY DAVID HU

HOUSE FOR A WAYFARER
(Re)considering the Meaning of PLACE in the Digital Age

As traveling becomes a common way of life, and more often to locations that are off the beaten path and more personal, clients and I have been sharing our memories of places: the food and wine of a place and the people, events, the sound and air, simple memories of a journey... And sometimes in-between places: the traveling itself, the airports, hotels, and cabins of planes or trains.

The client for the Sea Girt House is an avid world wide traveler and has homes in various locations. He once showed me his home in South America where you'd always find him for certain seasons. When we started the project, he said that the Sea Girt House would be his main home because he loves the place most. As the house is just about one hour's drive from New York City, this would be a place to show his hospitality.

This sharing of traveling conveys **senses of place**. In there is the **sense of Being** which to me is the foundation for the design of this project.

Instead of focusing on room sizes, shapes and arrangements, and what architectural features or exteriors/interiors should look or feel like, the question became what should be the 'place' that will complement (with its inner universe) and manifest (with its architecture) the sense of Being of the client.

As the client is a doctor and a wide-ranging writer, the image of a wayfarer entered my mind: his house should be a place of wandering, wayfaring. The house should be part of the natural terrain and setting, and most importantly, it should have an interior landscape to match the client's own.

Swimming is a refuge for him. In his youth he spent summers at the Jersey Shore as a lifeguard. There was a swimming pool room in his prior house. He once showed it to me. Its air and atmosphere were musky and suffocating. He said many times he wanted to swim but turned away upon opening the door. He also shared with me his affinity for Eastern thinking. A swimming/meditation pool as the heart of the house-landscape seemed most suited: this indoor pool needed to be out there with the ocean and the sky.

Landscape and wayfaring remind me of the Chinese literati landscape paintings. Chinese literati painting is a conceptual, mental place. It is derived from writing and has evolved into a screen of signifiers that speaks with the viewer through layers of abstract, symbolic representational systems: *it is a place in our cognitive space*.

Chinese literati painting is a sub-genre of Chinese painting but it has the deepest influence in the Chinese psyche. The iconic long scroll of Fu Chun, at 7 meters in length, was not realistically meant to be viewed in its entirety at once. It was meant to be "read" as one end unfurls and the other furls back correspondingly. The on-view portion of the painting is always the size of the space between a person's two arms and fits within a desk's surface, about 60 cm. The overall image is the amalgamated memories of the sections in the cognitive space: a mental place, a personal sense of place. The Sea Girt house invokes such a sense of place.

In Chinese literati painting the picture is executed with the brushwork that resembles, and is grounded in the technique of, calligraphy. The historical spatial concept of *liu-bai* that pivots Chinese literati arts is inherited from the blank space of calligraphy.

More importantly, in this tradition the *liu-bai* space acts uniquely as a spatial transition for signifiers of diverse disciplines to co-exist in the blank space. As the blank space can be surrounding a chop or blanketing the paper to represent clouds, mists, water all in one, it is a cognitive space which also suspends written texts: poetry, essay, attribution as well as chops. As an integral whole the correlated writing completes the visual composition of the painting; it

Travelogue from 30,000 ft.

Some thoughts on Fu Chun Tu 富春山居圖.

also adds the dimension of text/thoughts to the cognitive space of the painting: it opens the door for abstraction. The end product of a Chinese literati painting is the summation of layers of information-deciphering and meaning-extraction merged in the cognitive space: **a place in the cognitive space.**

Architecture abiding by and revealing the tectonics of their time, and placed in the context of cognitive space enriched by the client's living details, creates a sense of place, **a place in our cognitive space:** they invoke and convey a personal sense of Being.

Zoning and building codes always have the most impacts on the design at the start. The shape of this house is very much defined by the codes. The rectangle shape is the maximum coverage to get the most square-footage. Even the roof shape: three stories allowed on the ocean front half of the house, two stories for the street front half, and limited overall building height. The code here also requires roofs to maintain a 30% slope -- the townscape is regulated by this code. Our approach was to create one *roof* that is 30% slope on average. The steeper street front averaged out the flatter ocean side that has the 3rd floor master bedrooms to ensure unrestricted views and desired ceiling heights.

As the spatial ideas and organization became clear, I asked the client to think about walls. The house was conceived to have extraordinary flow of interconnected space that emphasizes spatial fluidity and constant movement of light, air and people. Should there be specific, desired locations to incorporate solid walls for hanging his art collections?

"I'd like this house itself to be a work of art, not a house in which to hang my art collections."

The result here is an avant garde house of the Digital Age with stainless steel roof, glass wall, aluminum rain-screen forming a two-to-three-story cathedral space, filled with ever-shifting natural light from a collection of unique skylights, that accommodate an interior landscape. The two 2nd floor courtyards bring in additional natural light for the western quarters of the house. They are called "the two lungs", as when their large glass doors are opened, they provide a profusion of natural ventilation for the cathedral space.

A house of its time: digital technologies worked with expert craftsmanship of long tradition.

The backbone of the building, its structure, was digitally manufactured in the shop down to every angle of the members, connecting plates and bolt holes. The entire system was then shipped to the site like a jigsaw puzzle set. It took the experienced workers just seven days to put it all together. There were nearly no identical pieces except for the row of 8 columns next to the glass curtain wall. Precision of this work was paramount as everything that follows depended on it.

The standing seam roof was manufactured based on the digitally designed roof layout but with all the folds and bending done on the site. As the folding lines were never perpendicular to the panels, every fold of the panels was manually executed against the carefully prepared substrates. All the cutouts for the irregularly shaped skylights were done with digital precision to their sizes, shapes, and locations on site. It was the collaboration of the long history of standing seam craftsmanship working with digital technology at the site.

The glass curtain wall and skylights were manufactured in China. More than half of the ground floor glass walls are 9' tall and 10' wide hurricane test-proofed sliding doors with heavy double-insulated, laminated glass panels. After traveling halfway around the world there was one chance for them to get it all right: to fit into the cutouts of the roof and with the building structure that supports the curtain wall – the entire east facade of the building facing the ocean.

This east facing glass wall is equipped with a shading system connected to the Lutron lighting and building system control that can be operated from anywhere with a smart phone. The entire underside of the roof is protected with high R-value spray-on insulation. The rain-screen covers the south and west walls adding significant protection against the elements and heat-gain from the sun.

A large fresh water pool in the middle of an open grand space generates considerable evaporation. The mechanical system was designed to capture the water in the air and recycle it back to the pool. The pool uses an ultra-violet disinfection system without chlorine so as not to emit unpleasant odors into the tranquil space.

Incorporating "the two lungs" for natural ventilation offsets the A/C load greatly: fresh air comes in through the large glass door openings on the first floor and out the two 2nd floor courtyards. Sea breezes are welcome here.

Memories of Steel.

The Beads of Skylights.

INTRODUCTION

BY BYRON HAWES

I've oft been heard to say, "Architecture is, in some ways, the most complicated and multivalent of creative pursuits." It's a métier that necessarily juxtaposes the precision of engineering and the poetry of sculpture.

An organism far transcending simple roof and walls; in furtherance of our purposes and evocative of our best intentions, rather than simply our need for shelter. A machine for living, as the maestro so famously said in "Vers une Architecture".

If we're honest, contemporary architecture has long-since transcended simple debates vis-à-vis form versus function, polymorphing into staggeringly layered explorations of environmental, physical, and material interactions with the very world in which we live.

And, at its best, a dense tapestry of functional, social, cultural, and historical tropes coalesce to form a near sentient physical entity.

The essence of Minimalism is simplicity, but simplicity without depth is merely cheap. It is not enough.
 - Ando Tadao

David Hu's Sea Girt House oscillates gracefully between a sort of proto minimalism and a hyper orchestrated spatial awareness.

"Minimalism" is a double-edged sword. Much as with a haiku or a classical violin solo, minimal design is complicated in that the fewer obvious elements the more perfectly composed those elements which exist must be. I also tend to find most categorizations of design and architecture as "minimalist" to be reductive and misleading. Taking Dieter Rams' famous principle of "As Little Design as Possible" literally is to miss utterly the point. Rather, Rams' point is to make complicated design decisions in the creation of a wholly functional and aesthetically minimal product that eschews all unnecessary adornments.

BYRON HAWES is a New York-based writer and designer. He is the founder of the underground design magazine *The Après Garde*, and a co-founder of I-V, a boutique architecture and design firm that has done projects including a recording studio for OVOsound, Campari's Canadian HQ, and Spin Toronto. He is contributing editor: architecture and design at Hypebeast, and previously served as a consulting editor at *Architectural Digest China*, as well as contributing to publications including *Monocle*, *Wallpaper*, *Apartamento*, and *Azure*, amongst others.

He has also authored or co-authored the books *We Are Wonderful: 25 Years of Design and Fashion in Limburg*, *The Landscape Architecture of Paul Sangha*, *Bedmar & Shi: In The Tropics*, *Post-Industrial Brutalism and the Daiquiri*, and several titles in ORO's Masterpiece Series.

Much as with the famous archi-ideological battle between the "Whites" (also known as the New York Five – Peter Eisenman, Michael Graves, John Hejduk, Richard Meier, and Charles Gwathmey) and the "Grays" (the Venturi, or Pop Architects – Allan Greenberg, Romaldo Giurgola, Jaquelin Robertson, Charles Moore, and Robert Stern), which nominally centred around a battle between simplicity and complexity, architectural pundits sometimes compartmentalize the idea of minimalism, and forget that all architects, at least in theory, are focused primarily on marrying their chosen aesthetic with functionality.

All this by way of saying that while upon first glance someone may make the mistake of identifying the interiors of David Hu's Sea Girt House as "minimalistic", I believe this inaccurate. While it does, peripherally, appear to be a masterclass in articulated subtlety, this is a byproduct of a broader goal. To produce a space that transcends functionality and livability, and achieves spirituality and a sense of holistic calm.

Exterior view, street side; Sea Girt House.

Sand dunes ashore of the Sea Girt House.

Partial exterior view, street side: Sea Girt House.

Space has always been the spiritual dimension of architecture. It is not the physical statement of the structure so much as what it contains that moves us.
- Arthur Erickson

The Sea Girt lies along a stretch of beachfront on the New Jersey shores in Monmouth County.

A staggering 11,000 sq/f (10,300 sq/m) of house, on a 26,000 sq/f (2,400 sq/m) lot, the glass, stainless steel, and concrete home is somehow simultaneously a whisper and a monster.

From the street, it's almost imposing. A highly angular façade of blue stucco and steel sheeting; somehow both mid-century and intensely futuristic. Richard Neutra meets Æon Flux.

Sufficiently sturdy that when Superstorm Sandy ravaged the east coast in 2012, during construction, with such force that a half-inch solid steel plate for the foot bridge over the pool was mangled beyond recognition, and the pool and basement were filled with 109 metric tons of sand, the structure itself remained undamaged.

And yet, when viewed from the beach, the house presents as an entirely different animal. A towering, three story sheet of glass. Completely open to its environment and surroundings. Collectively, the two façades provide insight into the house's impetus. It's a sanctuary. A private oasis. Unapologetic about its mission statement; to provide an entirely private and personal respite from society, while still maintaining maximum proximity and interaction with the environment.

The house boasts three stories, six bedrooms, and an elevator, and yet somehow feels almost unencumbered by the typical breakdown of a residence. As though the entire space is completely open; indifferent to traditional spatial breakdowns, and even the concept of 'rooms' itself.

A completely open plan ground floor is centred around a rectangular in-ground swimming pool-cum-water feature, crossed by a glass bridge, which delineates between living spaces and library at one end, and an all-white Boffi kitchen, pantry, and dining areas at the other.

The second floor, which can be accessed via the glass elevator or an awe-inspiring staircase of exposed steel and glass risers, houses four bedroom suites and two interior courtyards; one of which is a water garden, while the other is one of vegetation, with walls of the palest, almost Barragánian or Sottsassian, pink.

The third story is split between two towering master suites, each replete with en-suite facilities and full views of the beach and shore. The master bathroom also features full-height glazing and an oversized Spoon Tub by Agape, allowing the occupant unfettered views of the beach but utter privacy. Make no mistake, this is more than a house; it is literally the calm in the storm.

I hope to achieve simplicity, but I also hope to achieve depth...I believe it is important that architecture should be a space where you feel spiritually empowered.
- Ando Tadao

I spoke at length with David Hu in the conceptualization of, and preparation for, this essay, with topics ranging from sense memory to tone poetry, from aesthetic imperatives to cross-cultural architectural histories.

But the conversations kept returning to David Hu's conception of this project as something substantially broader. A sense of more than just a space; but one of a "place." Of something spiritual. Secular, to be sure, in the conventional sense, but ritualistic. Holistic.

Seashore.

Exterior panel detailing; Sea Girt House.

Hu spoke at length of his relationship, his interactions, with the commissioning client; a published psychiatrist turned cinema screenwriter. Of how blessed he felt to have a client who chose not to dictate specifics, but rather to simply get to know one another; to discuss things that mattered to both of them, in the assumption that by engaging in a discourse about life, and not simply architecture, a path would present itself.

We discussed Richard Strauss' Four Last Songs. Those which the Houston Symphony once referred to as the Metaphysical Sunset. Strauss' elegiac swan song. Of Hu's curious association between that particular piece of music and this project. An embodiment not only of reminiscence, or of geo-locational sense memory, but also of a curiously familiar chord progression and tonality. Of his understanding of the Four Last Songs as a deceptively honest piece; which, while meandering or wandering through various themes and progressions, inevitably returns to a major key.

Hu spoke of how it continuously reminds him of this house. A place that provides the space and impetus to continue to wander. And not just wander, but soar. And, yet, around every corner the keystone; the major key; the horizon, re-emerges. More light. More perspective. More...opportunity.

Church architecture describes visually the idea of the sacred, which is a fundamental need of man.
- Mario Botta

This house is not a church. In any sense. But theism presumes only the existence of "God," in whatever form, not a specificity of what God means. I choose not to debate with any person their definition of God, and thank others not to debate with me mine. And I take no compunction in using the holiest of words to vaguely describe a feeling, or an ideal. Personally whatever God is has manifested to me most clearly in the first time I visited Ando's Church of the Light, and the first time I read Maugham's *The Razor's Edge*. I'm assuming that this experience varies greatly. And I mean no disrespect.

But it is clear that there was some manner of holy intention in the conceptualization and construction of this house. The interior's central nodal point, the water feature/swimming pool, is far more than would instinctively be assumed. Centrally situated, perpendicular to the shore, and mirrored/combatted by a long diamond-shaped skylight directly above it, the pool takes an instinctive center stage.

If the house's central exterior environmental focus – the beach/skyline/waterfront – is the altar, then the pool is the transept. At certain times of day, standing on the glass bridge that spans the pool, one cannot avoid the sense that the light is...different. Otherworldy. Gothic. Even...dare I...holy. As with the aforementioned Church of the Light, a sense is provided of an entity being created entirely of a provided perspective of natural light.

When I first began to speak with Mr. Hu, we spoke of many things, one of which was his Taiwanese heritage. And of how the creations of artists remains a mysterious thing to said artists. Because, if we're honest, that which has come before us will always imbue that which we do later. Artists, be they architects, composers, painters, what have you, will invariably create based on the sum total of information and experience that their life has, thus far, drawn them through. Much will be intentional. And, equally, much will be subconscious. As our conversation progressed down this line, I was abstractly reminded of a masterful Taiwanese film, *What Time is it There?*, from the iconic director Tsai Ming-lian. A profoundly dense film, which has drawn comparisons to the works of Ozu, Bresson, and Antonioni. I would provide a synopsis of the plot, but, as with many "serious" works of art, the more words I endeavored to use, the less I would likely wind up saying.

Horizon viewed from 3rd floor bridge.

There is a continuous theme, however, which revolves around time. Much as with the early works of Wong Kar Wai (particularly *Days of Being Wild*), time is an elusive mistress. Fleeting; floating; ethereal; and immutable. Characters experience similar or opposing realities simultaneously. One flees her native Taipei for Paris, with no particular purpose. Things continue to happen both disparately and coincidently. Writing about the film, Ebert said "The movie then develops into a story that seems to involve synchronicity, but actually involves our need for synchronicity. We need to believe that our little lives are in step with distant music, when synchronicity is simply the way coincidence indulges itself in wish-fulfillment."

Our compositions are comprised of a million little things. Obsessions and distant memories. Fragments and focal points. And, by "our," I include not only creators but creations.

Take that swimming pool, for example. In a lesser structure, it would be referred to as a water feature, and justifiably so. But, in this house, it is the culmination of a broad series of signifiers. A response to the majesty of the shoreline opposite. An acknowledgement of the client's love of swimming, and of the (discussed in the architect's introduction) reality of his previous..for lack of a better word..hangups about the in-house swimming pool at a previous residence. A cognizant appreciation for the client's spiritual aspirations; manifesting as a deeply contemplative meditation pool.

Be truthful. Nature only sides with truth.
- Adolf Loos

As with most artfully crafted private residences blessed with a natural setting literally beyond the whims or wiles of man, the Sea Girt House sees a clear responsibility in honouring the horizon beyond, and the environment without.

The house's roof is a byzantine composition of positive and negative spaces; awash in Libeskindian skylights, of such frequency that no mistake can be made with regards to the seeking of allowing the house's surrounding environment every opportunity of permeating every nook and cranny.

The expansive, and panoramic, ground floor was finished in white epoxy, which literally reflects the abundant natural light throughout the space; coating it in the very external beauty that inspired its existence.

Nearly every component of the central living space (including master bedrooms, and all communal spaces, living, dining, and so on) are spatially situated in such a way that the panoramic view of the horizon beyond is centrally featured. As mentioned, this extends to the master bathrooms, where floor-to-ceiling glazing allows full views of the shore beyond, even while engaging in the most private of behaviors.

Nowhere is this more crystallinely demonstrated than in the kitchen, where the far wall (which incorporates Miele fixtures) is composed entirely of black lacquer. A reflective surface, as are most in the house, if one stops to consider it. An intentional ode to that same magnificent horizon, and a tacit nod to the fact that the house is utterly comprised around its glory. Even while facing directly away from the shore, and while engaging in the most quotidian of activities (pulling an espresso, or dropping a stuffed chicken in the oven) one is both consciously and unconsciously confronted by the naked beauty of the horizon beyond.

With this specific feature I was reminded of the Impressionists habit of staring deeply into a black mirror, periodically, while engaged in the act of painting. With the assumption and intention that by doing so their aesthetic neutrality would be rediscovered. A mid-meal lemon sorbet, for the eye, as it were.

Small touches of this nature are the difference between a house, and an icon. Between good, and great, design. Between a pursuit and a calling. Seemingly innocuous, but, ultimately, representative of a much broader exploration.

Collage compostition view from top floor private rooms.

We Don't Embroider Cushions Here.
- Le Corbusier

With a space this, to be frank, absurdly large, and absurdly aesthetic, interior design could easily present a problem. Fortunately, the commissioning client was possessed of the inspiration, and palate, to honour the structure.

A not insignificant contemporary art collection, and a long-standing relationship with Murray Moss, proprietor of the legendary (and now defunct) eponymous design space in New York City's SoHo district, led to a furnishing equal parts playful, inspired, and articulate. Iconic pieces from designers including the Campana Brothers, Maarten Baas, Studio Job, and Edra parse the space, solidifying a tactility and livability, while simultaneously complementing the house itself.

I don't believe architecture has to speak too much. It should remain silent and let nature in, in the guise of sunlight and wind.
- Ando Tadao

Ultimately, the Sea Girt House is, for all these words, less an enigma and more an entity.

A deeply contemplative odyssey. A highly environmentally filial endeavour. A project that makes no bones about its purpose of providing a single-minded solitude for its inhabitant, even while demonstrating its unwavering solicitude towards its surrounding environment.

Beach houses are always meant to provide a combination of comfort, security, and beauty. But rarely do they do so with this level of articulation.

This house, if we're honest, is inviting on the surface, but endlessly gifted with surprises. Small details, and thoroughly intentional minor features, that clearly demonstrate the difference between "art," and art.

WALK THROUGH
BY BYRON HAWES

The Morning Ritual

Part of David Hu's aesthetic dialogue with regards to the design of this house revolved around creating a lyrical, and winsome, morning meander to the kitchen; encompassing and experiencing both the architecture and natural environment that makes this place so special.

His introduction to the perfect morning stroll from bed to breakfast is below, and accompanied by a pictoral progression on the opposing page.

The client indicated that one of his most important morning rituals is the trip from his bedroom to the kitchen. My response was to make that trip the longest circulation path in the house:

"You'd perch at the side of your bed staring at the horizon and the breaking waves while the dreams slowly fade away. Standing up with the thought of a fresh cup of coffee, you'd turn towards the bedroom door and walk across the first bridge right outside with the horizon still lingering beyond the side of the bridge. You'd arrive at the top of the straight stairs (the 2nd bridge) crossing the swimming pool two floors below, walk down and arrive at the bamboo garden courtyard on the second floor – one of the two lungs (two 2nd floor exterior gardens) of the house. Watching the glistening of the leaves and hearing the ruffling sound of the bamboo in the morning breeze, you'd turn and cross the long, 3rd bridge of the second floor towards the end of the bridge where the sculptural main stair meets the water garden courtyard, the other lung. You'd turn and stroll down the main stair (the 4th bridge) where the glass curtain wall fills your sight and the entire horizon stretches across the glass veil. You'd arrive at the living room where all the wine glasses and cheese plates are scattered with the sound of music and laughter still lingering in the air. You'd maneuver towards the swimming/meditation pool, cross the glass bridge over the tranquil water and stand by the dining table when the smell of coffee overtakes your senses. You'd have another glance at the now golden horizon, and just a few more steps, you will have arrived at the kitchen.

Yes, there is the other easier, shorter, and faster, route to this trip: take the elevator. Though different, but the experience is exhilarating in its own way. You'd be descending in a glass cabin with the slowly moving view of the horizon and the waves of the beach front across the expanse of the glass wall."

DESIGN

DESCRIPTION

To move beyond the restrictions in the conventional realms of an architect's services, a few of them need to be subverted:

1) Client/architect relationship

Conventionally, a clear agreement is set at the beginning of a project on the program/requirements to establish the client's and architect's mutual-understanding: the agreed upon "program". However, the architect must assist the client to explore a broader dimension of his program.

In the case of the Sea Girt House, the client came with very few requirements: "I need 7 bedroom suites," he said, "two Master suites on the third floor, three children's suites and one guest suite on the second, and one maid's suite on the first floor. I want an indoor swimming pool that is not in an enclosed "swimming pool room." Period.

An unusually simple "program" to work with required a leap of faith from both parties.

"I acquired this property ten years ago. After all these years living in my many homes, I'd like this place to be my main home. Surprise me." Carte blanche is a double-edged sword.

For the Sea Girt House the first step was to deconstruct "function" so as to dislodge from the restrictions of the conventional notion of "function": to reconsider it by re-defining the thematic nature of the house. Function was about purpose for Being rather than specifically designated usages.

The key example, with the full awareness of the gravity of the pool for this project demanded the reconsideration of the purpose of the pool rather than narrowly defining its use. For this project this water feature had to be a swimming/landscape/meditation pool all at once that formed the core of *sense of place* for the house and connected with the client physically and spiritually.

A landscape that is connected with "re-imagined bridges" and networks of pathways that's punctuated with arching sculptural stairs was conceived to accomplish this vision.

Then the theme of the house emerged: a place for a wayfarer, a micro-cosmos that inspires wandering, wayfaring and to connect with the macro-cosmos outside.

With the theme developed, new references as sub-themes

became clear to set the tone for tectonics that underscored the "sense of place:" the Horizon, the sky and light, the bridges, the lungs and the cathedral space. These themes ultimately informed the expression of the architecture, and became the "functions" that made the house.

A small matter that was important to the client: perhaps a balcony could be created with a shower, so it would be possible to enjoy snow falling on the head while showering. This was a thought in sync with the purpose of the house, but a balcony? My response was to have one of the master showers under an operable skylight, and in coordination with a large glass panel of the curtain wall next to the skylight also operable and slides to the side.

2). Design/communication techniques.

Realign design processes and dialogue within the design team and with the client.
Reformat study and presentation within the team and to the client.
Studies were no longer only sketches on the yellow tracing paper:
Rhyno wire frame studies and renderings, superimpositions, layering, cut-and-pasting of rendering studies and other visual elements, mixture of rendering/photograph and CAD images: to capture *senses of place* by subverting the preciseness of digital tools.

3) Incorporate construction into an inter-weaving design/realization process.

Cross-purposing construction documents as well as shop drawings as design drawings. Make this the last defense not to only ensure the correctness of execution but also to review if the design intention will be fully manifested when built.

Digital technologies have started unprecedented social and cultural changes and impacted our collective sense of Being in every imaginable way. In order to open new possibilities that explore paths for humanity and pivots for our senses of Being, conventional notions of architectural "practice" must be deconstructed – and not just by utilizing the digital tools. This re-thinking has to happen in all aspects of the practice, from architect/client dynamics down to design process, presentations, and methods of realization, so as to re-focus the purpose of architecture and its role in the evolution of humanity.

STUDIES & PRESENTATION DRAWINGS

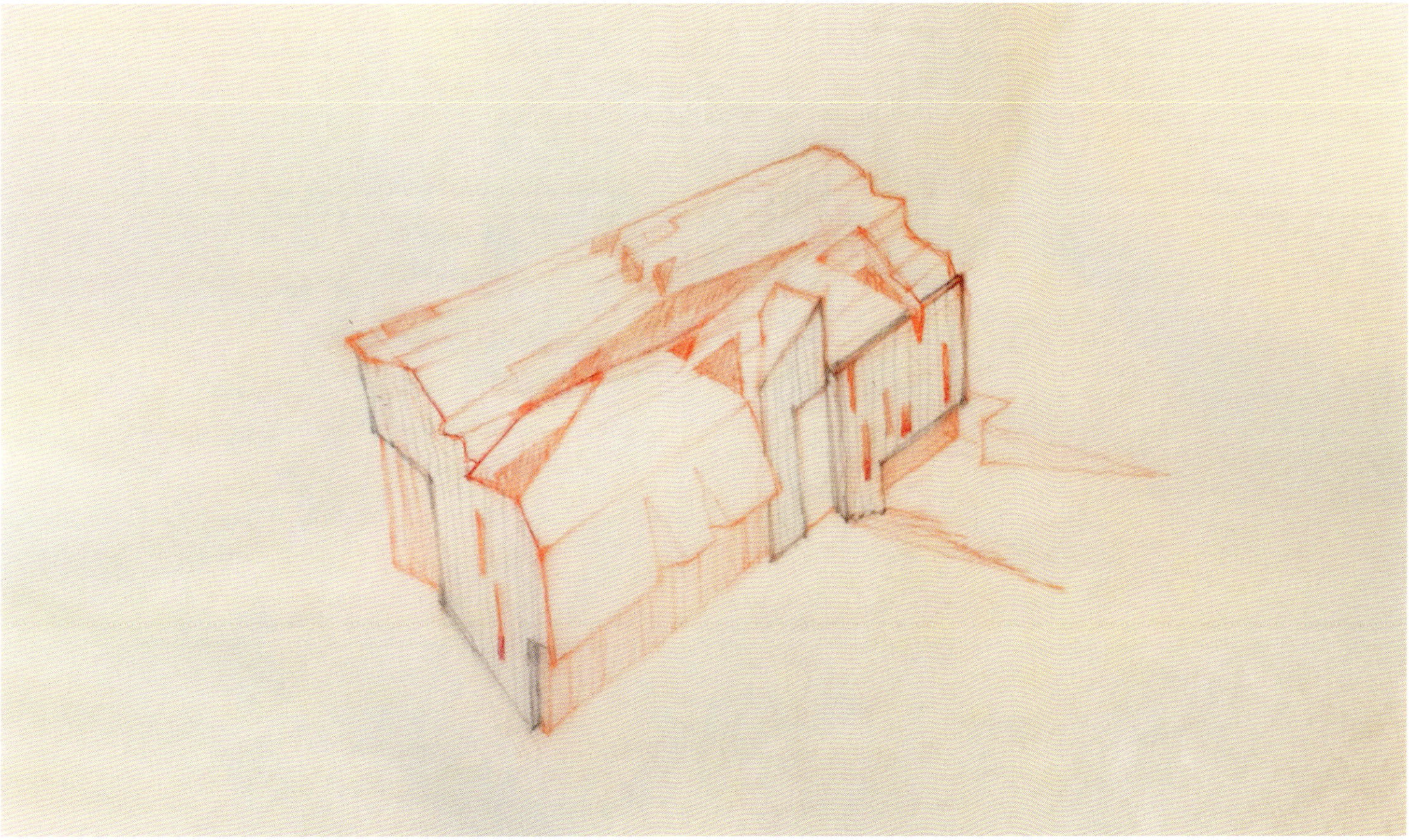

Volumetric Study

Early Hand Sketch of the Roof

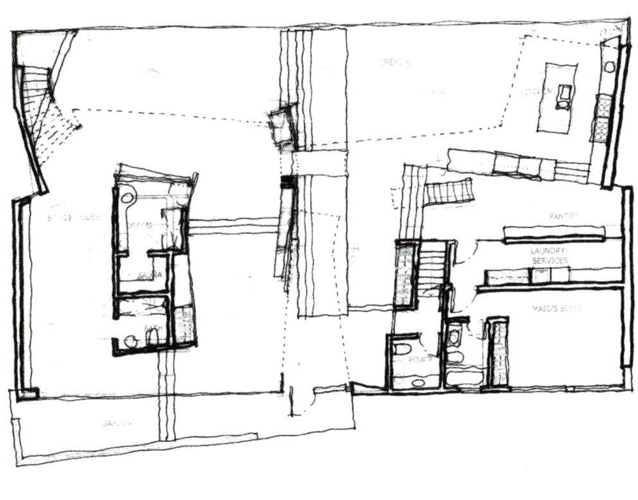

Early Plan Scheme

Google View of Site

Site Plan

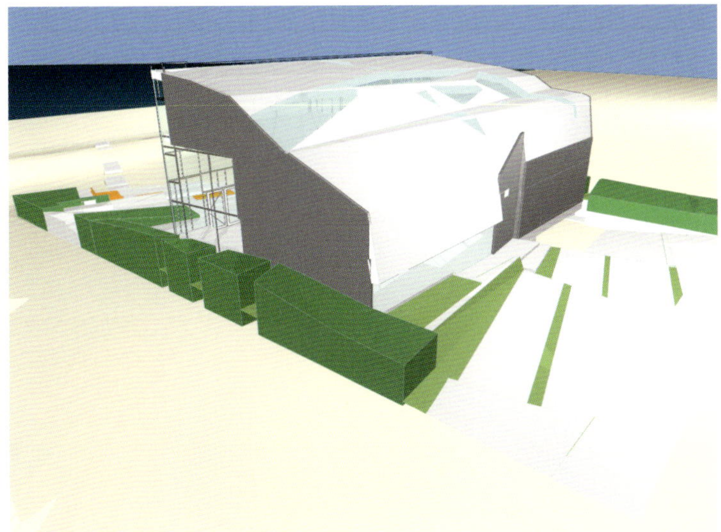

3D Perspective

View of East Yard

East Yard Landscape

3D Perspective

Night View Study

Bookshelf from Atrium

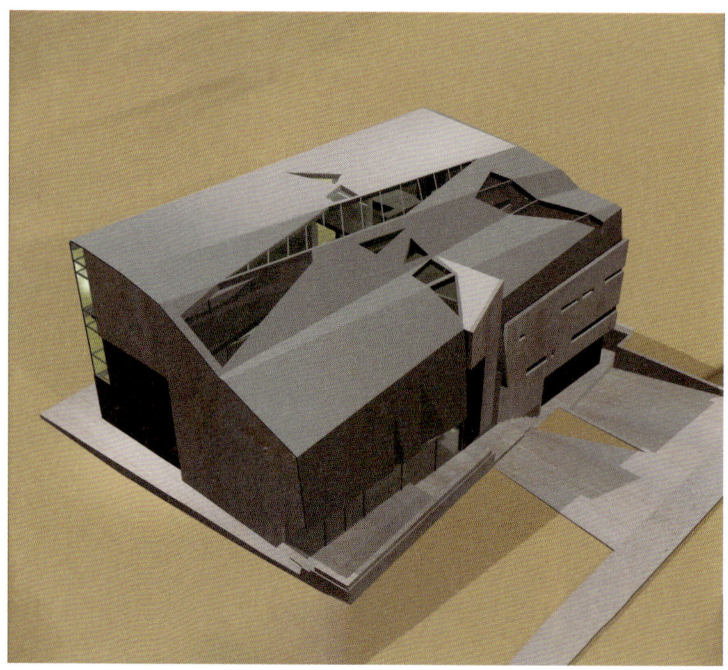

3D Perspective

Glass Curtain Wall Studios

Glass Curtain Wall Studios

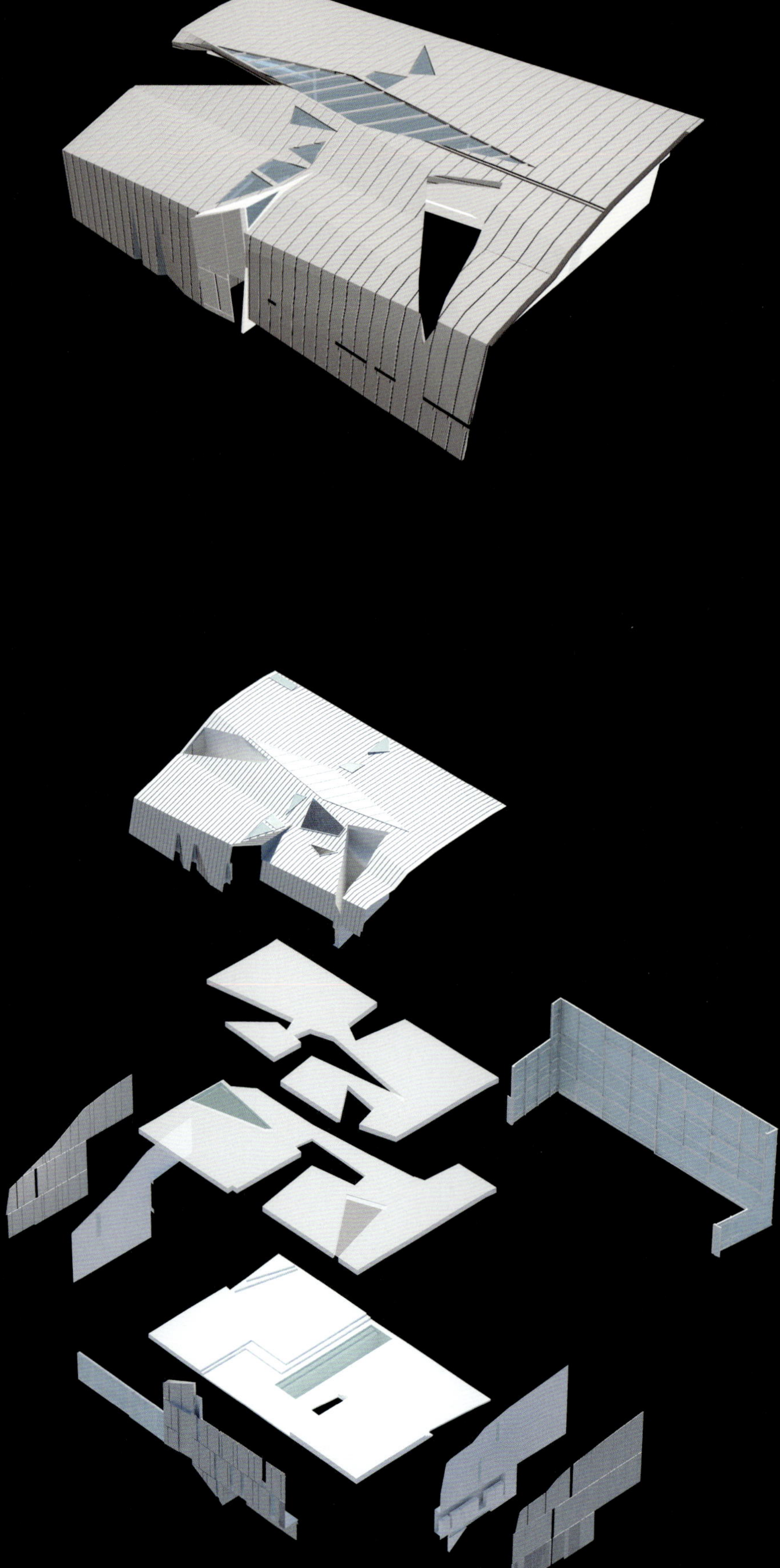

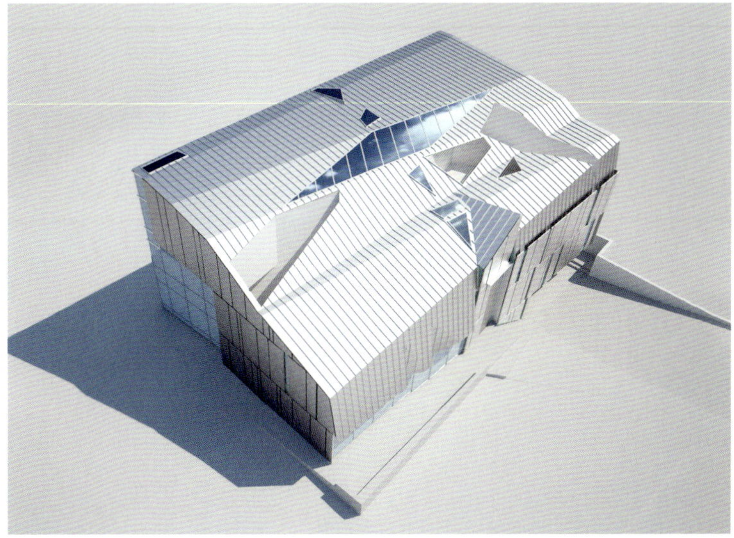

3D Perspective

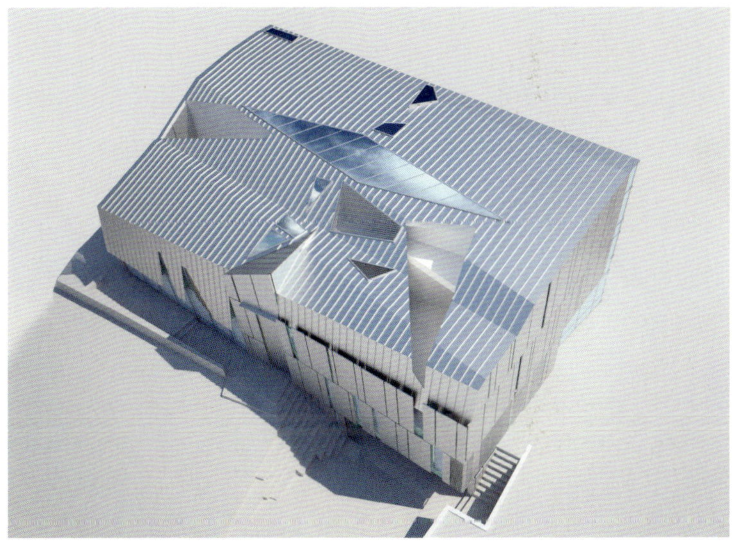

3D Perspective

3D Perspective

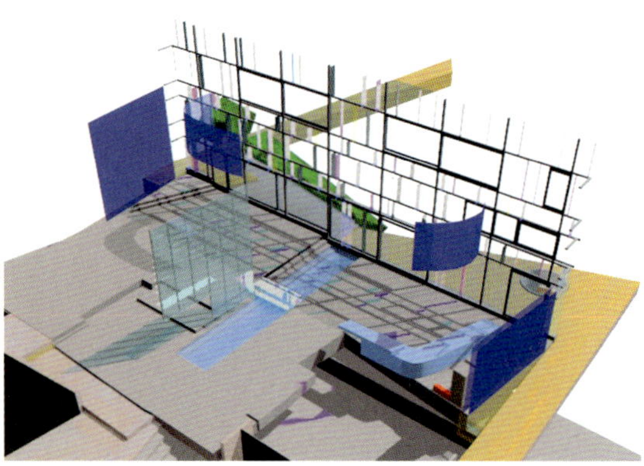

Main Space Study

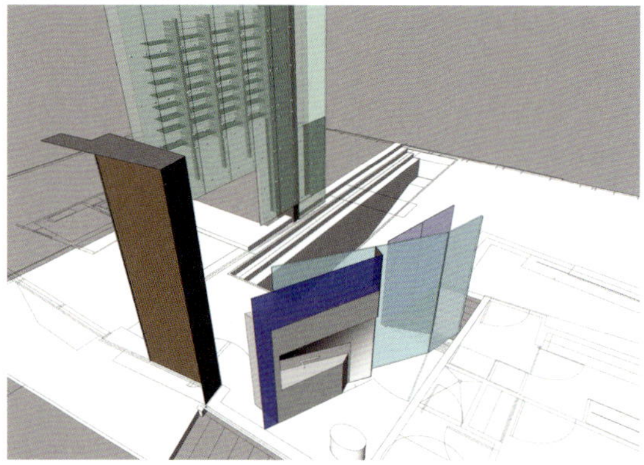

Entry Study

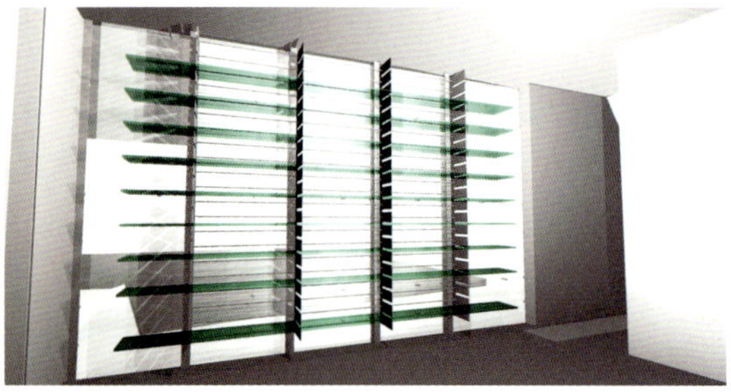

Bookshelf Study

Bookshelf Study

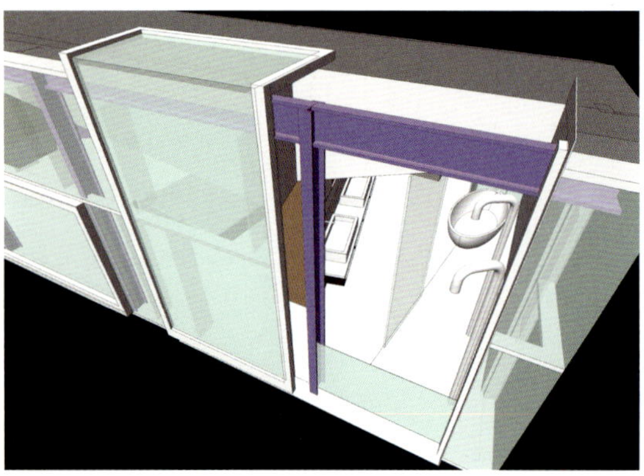

Master Shower Skylight Study

Master Shower Skylight Study

Upper Stair

Main Stair

Upper Stair

Main Stair

Main Stair

Main Stair

1- Entrance
2- Vestibule
3- Library
4- Two-Way Fireplace
5- GL Elevator
6- Sculptural Stair
7- Living
8- GL Bridge
9- Pool
10- Dining
11- Kitchen
12- Pantry
13- Service
14- Maid's Suite
15- Ramp to Garage

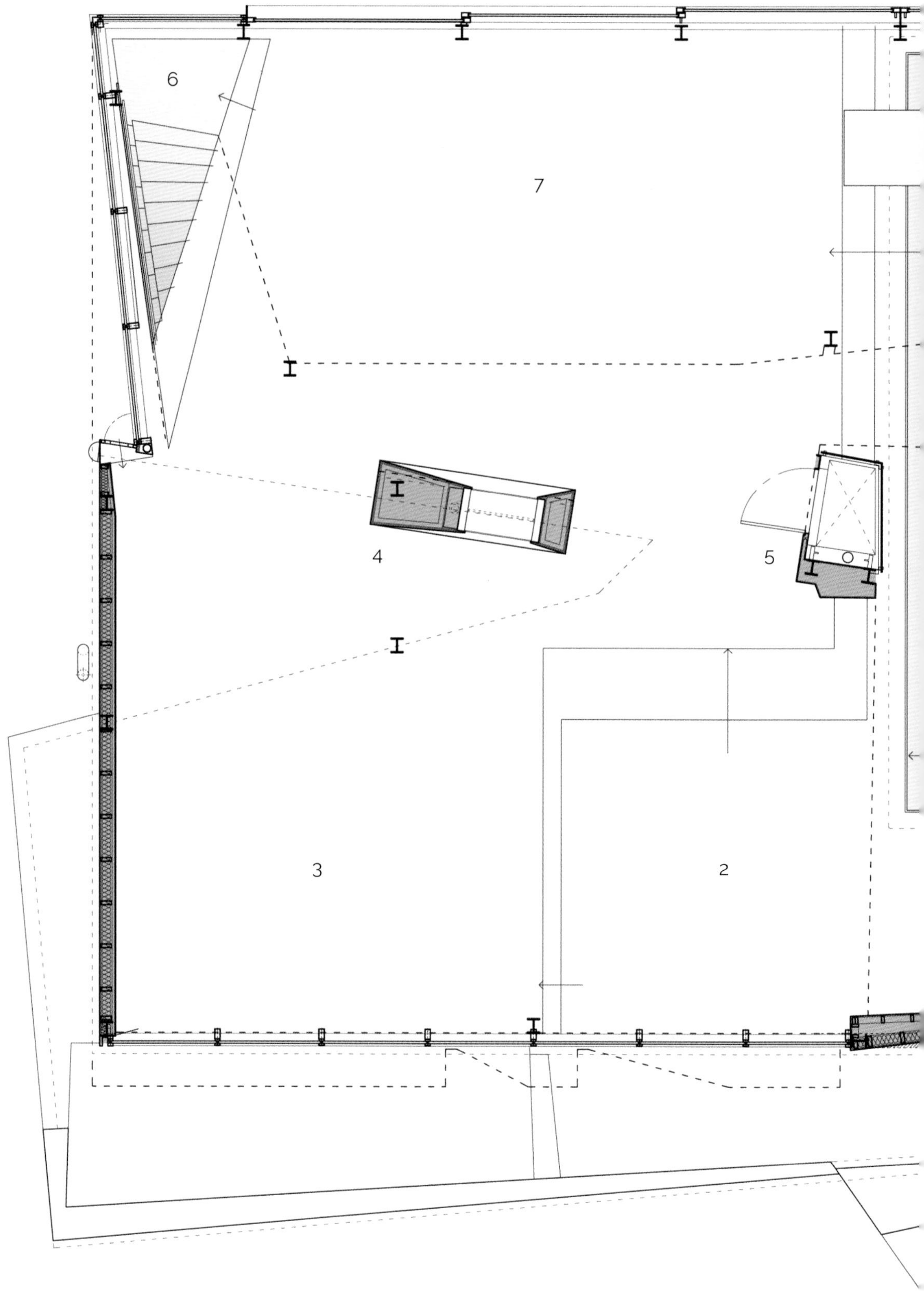

Ground Floor

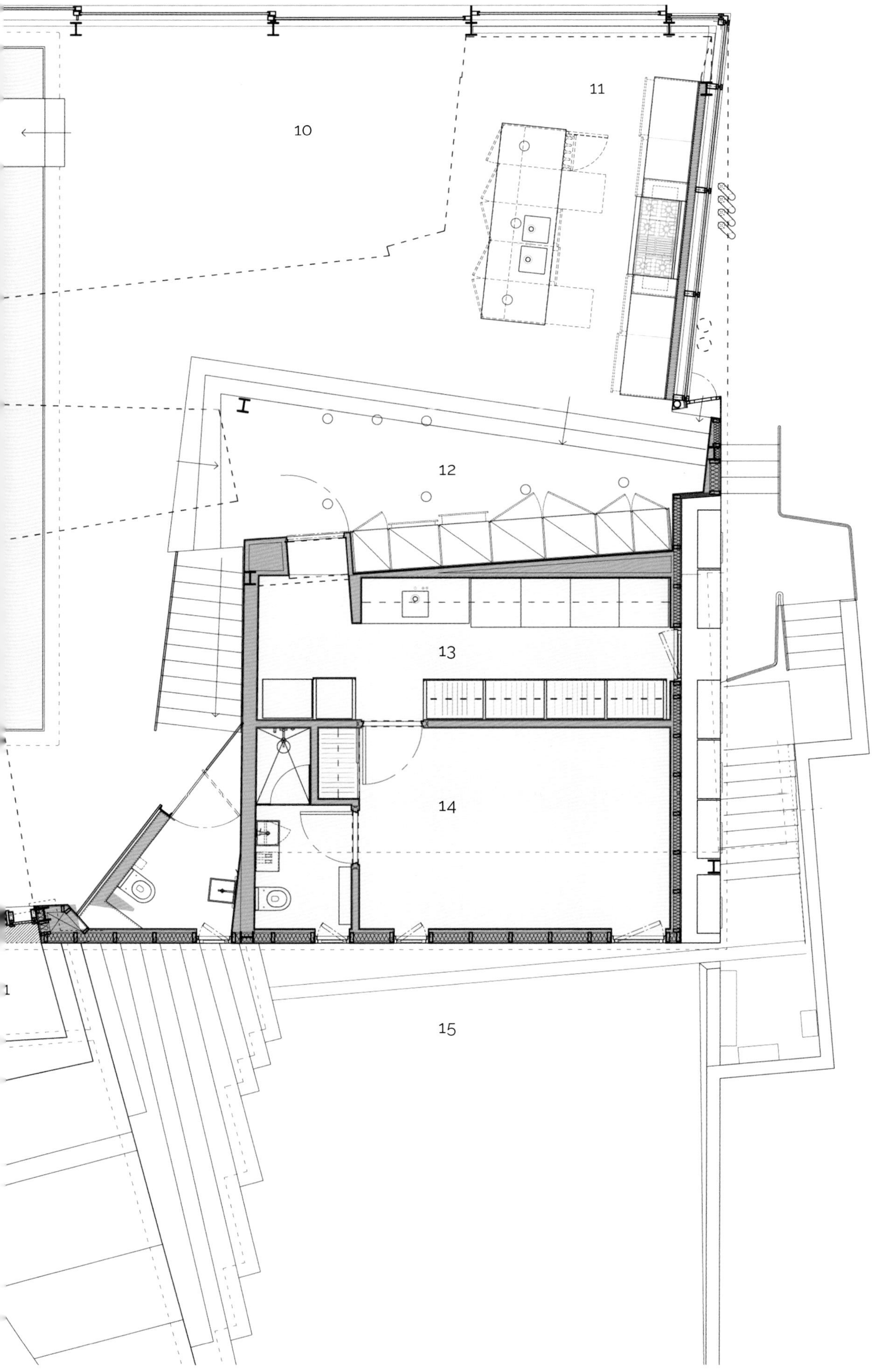
10
11
12
13
14
15
1

16- Open
17- Den/Br 2
18- Br 1
19- Courtyard
20- Open
21- Bridge
22- Br 3
23- Courtyard
24- Guest

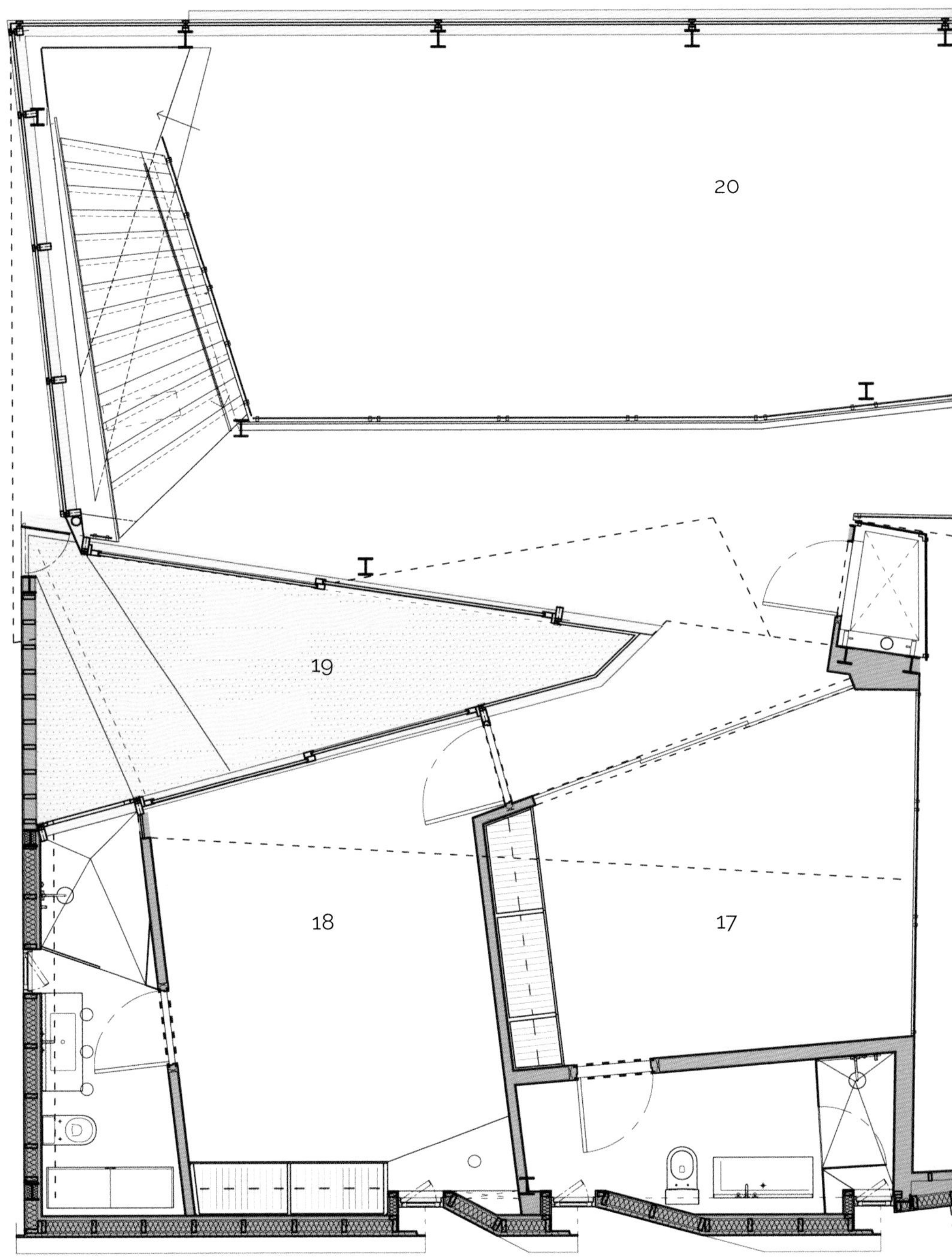

Second Floor

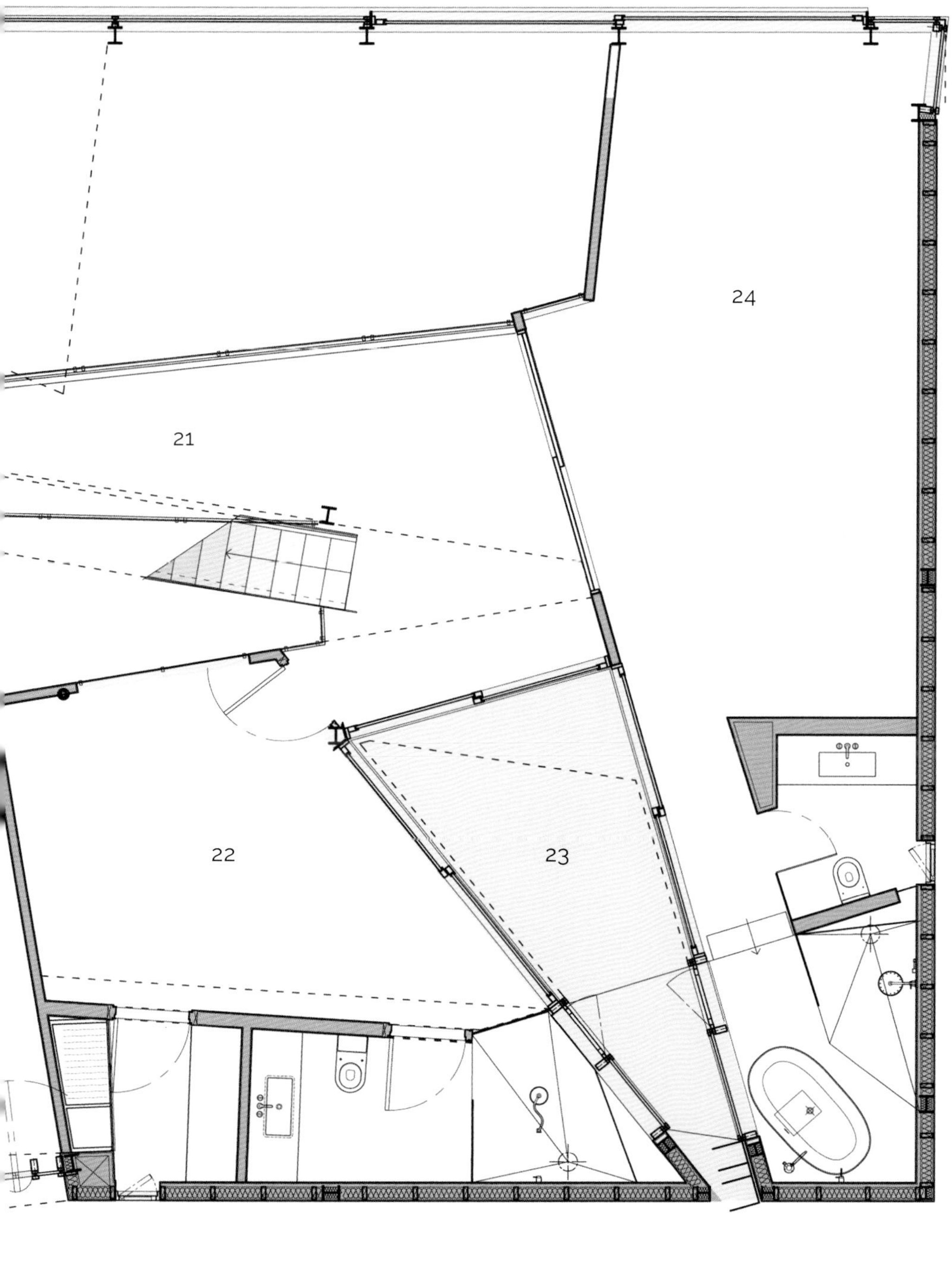
24
21
22
23

25- Open
26- Mechanical
27- Open
28- Master Br 1
29- Open
30- Master Br 2
31 - Open
32- Shoe Cl

Third Floor

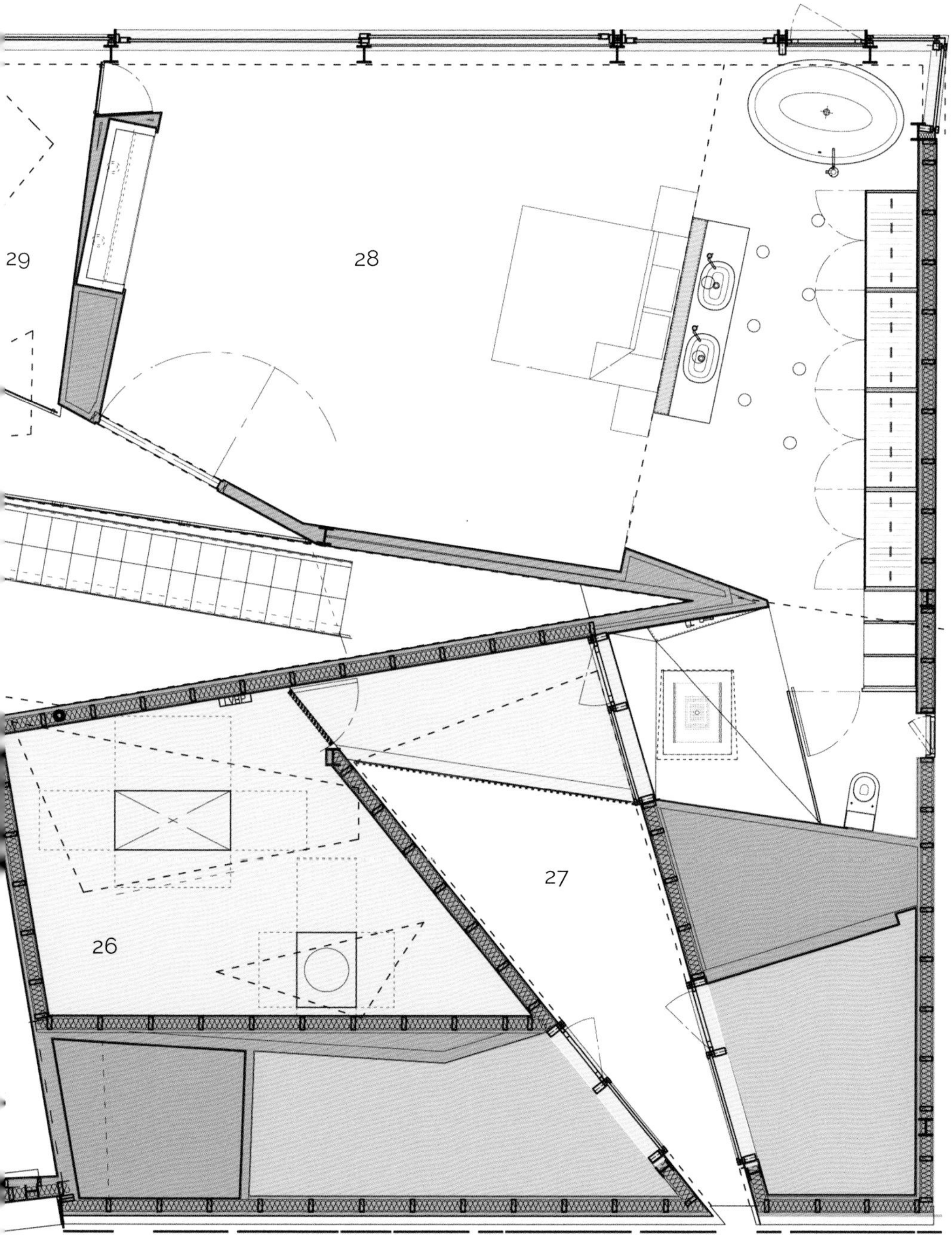
29
28
27
26

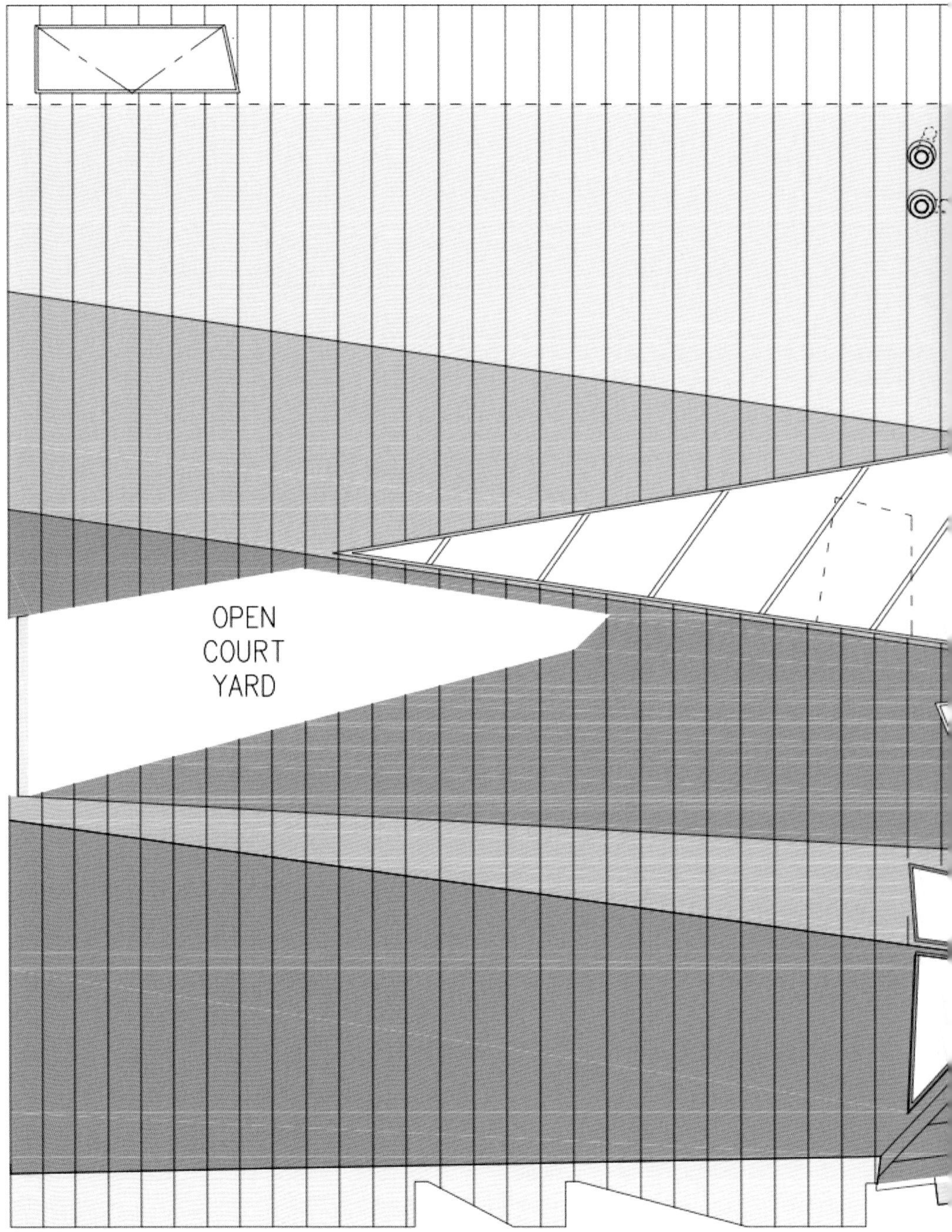

Roof Plan

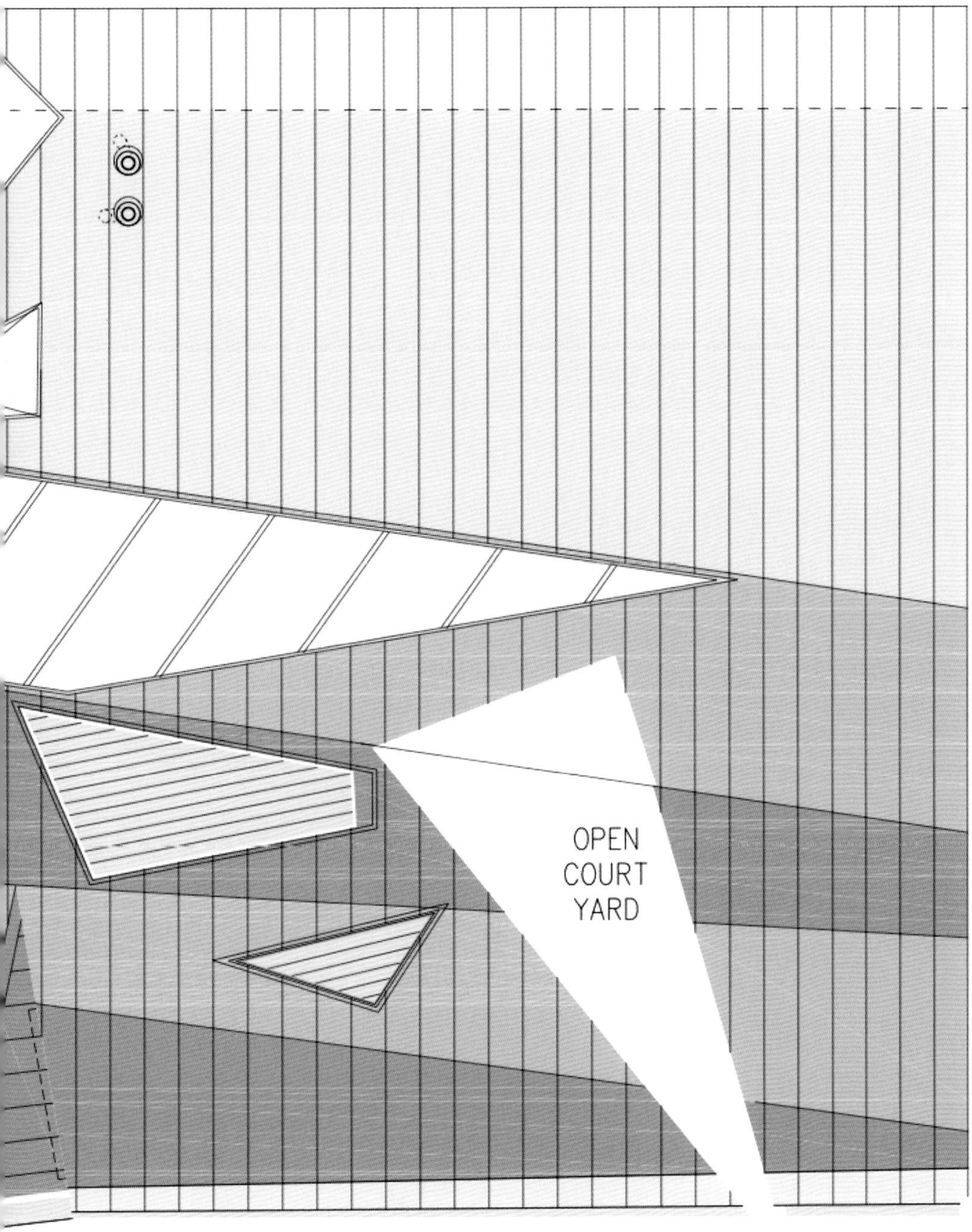
OPEN
COURT
YARD

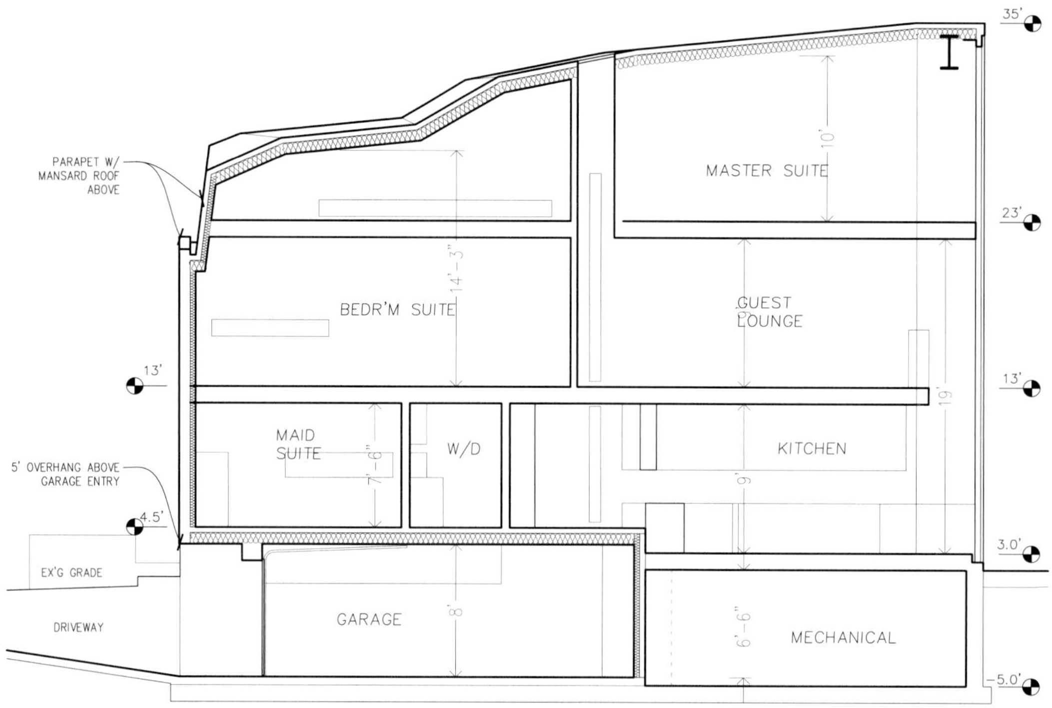

5
A4.0
NORTH CROSS SECTION @ GARAGE & LOT
SCALE: 3/16"=1'-0"

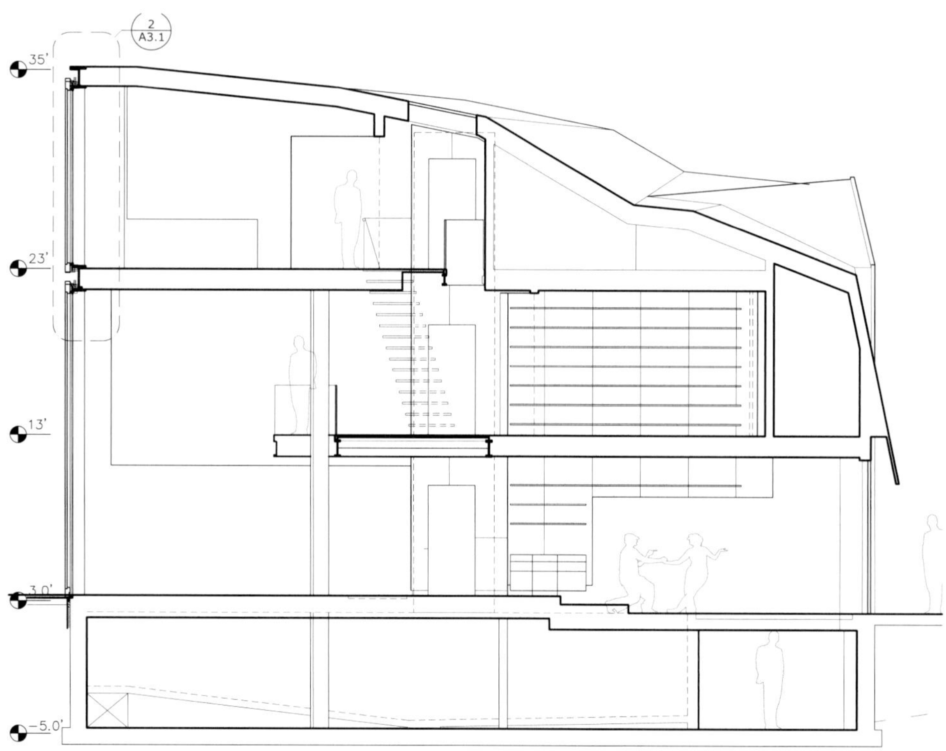

3
A4.0
SOUTH CROSS SECTION @ DEN
SCALE: 3/16"=1'-0"

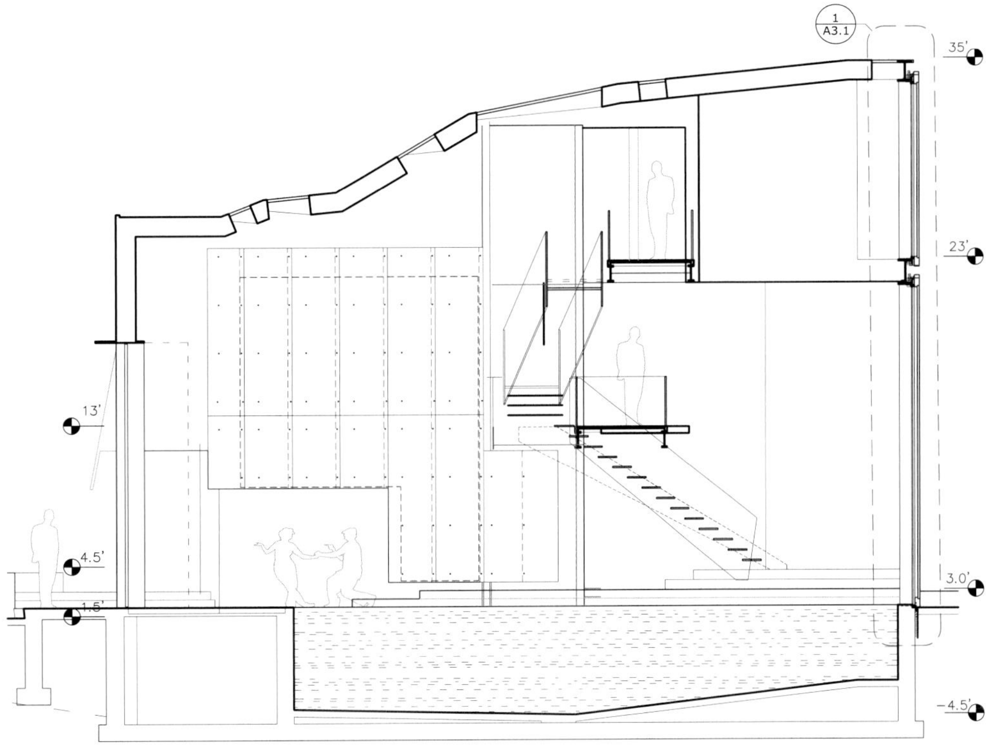

4 NORTH CROSS SECTION @ POOL
A4.0 SCALE: 3/16"=1'-0"

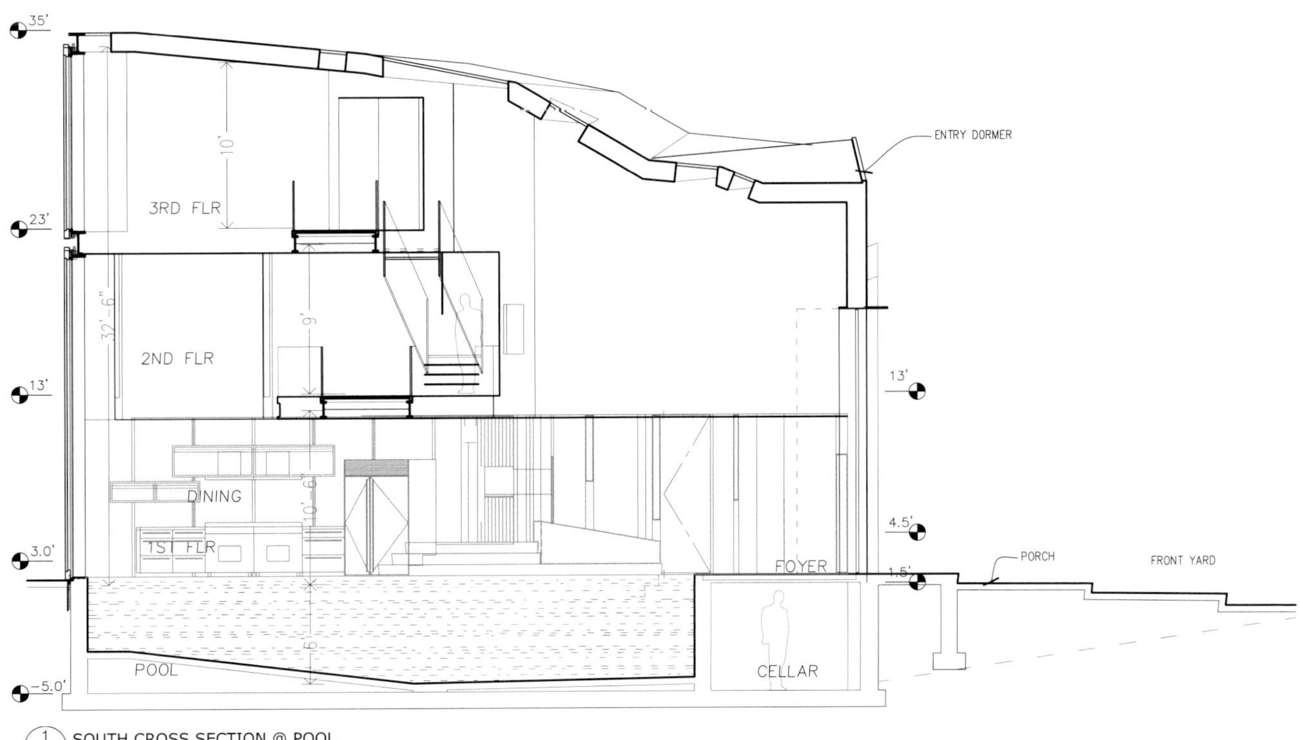

1 SOUTH CROSS SECTION @ POOL
A4.0 SCALE: 3/16"=1'-0"

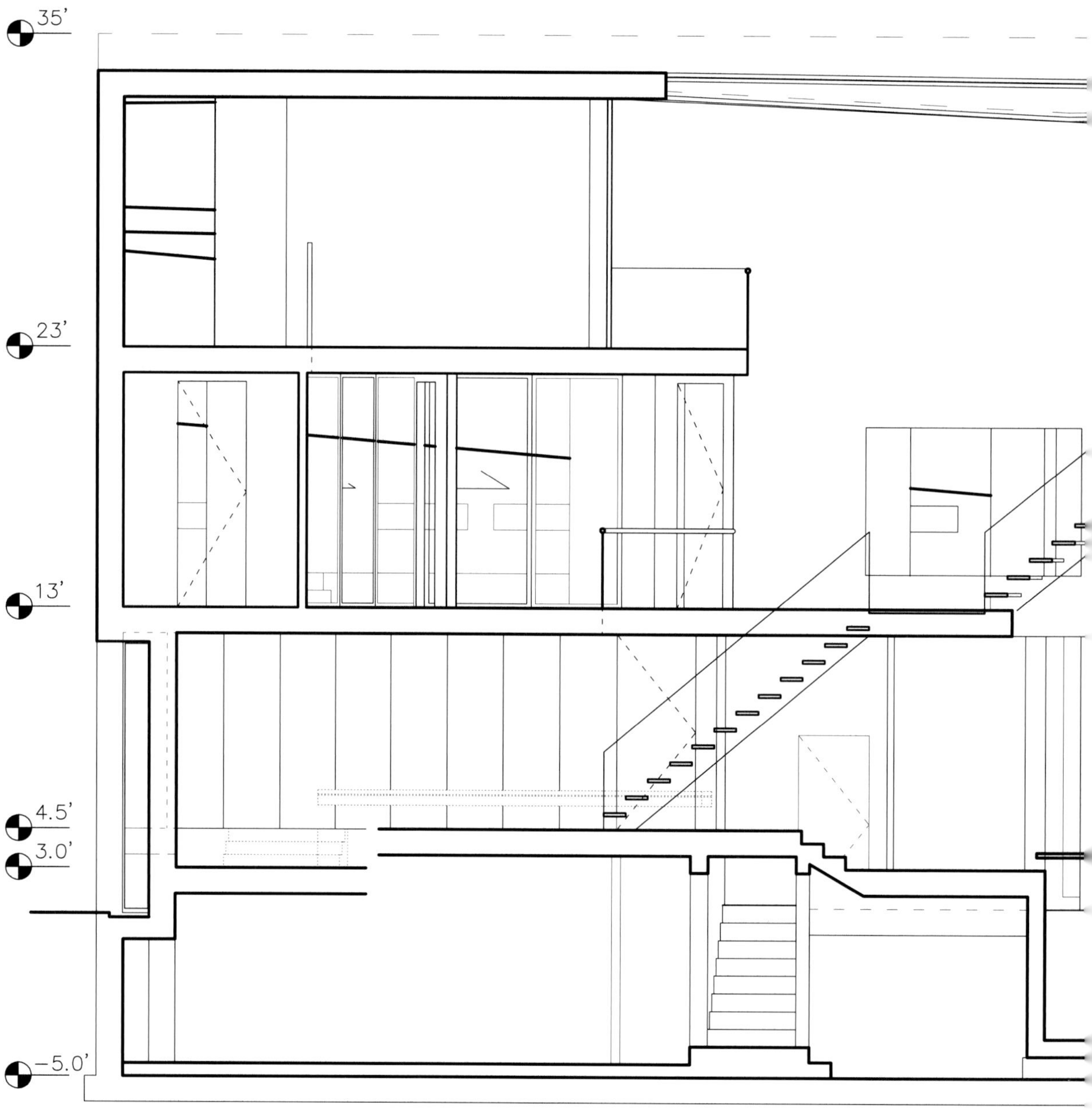

2 A4.0 **LONG SECTION**
SCALE: 3/16"=1'-0"

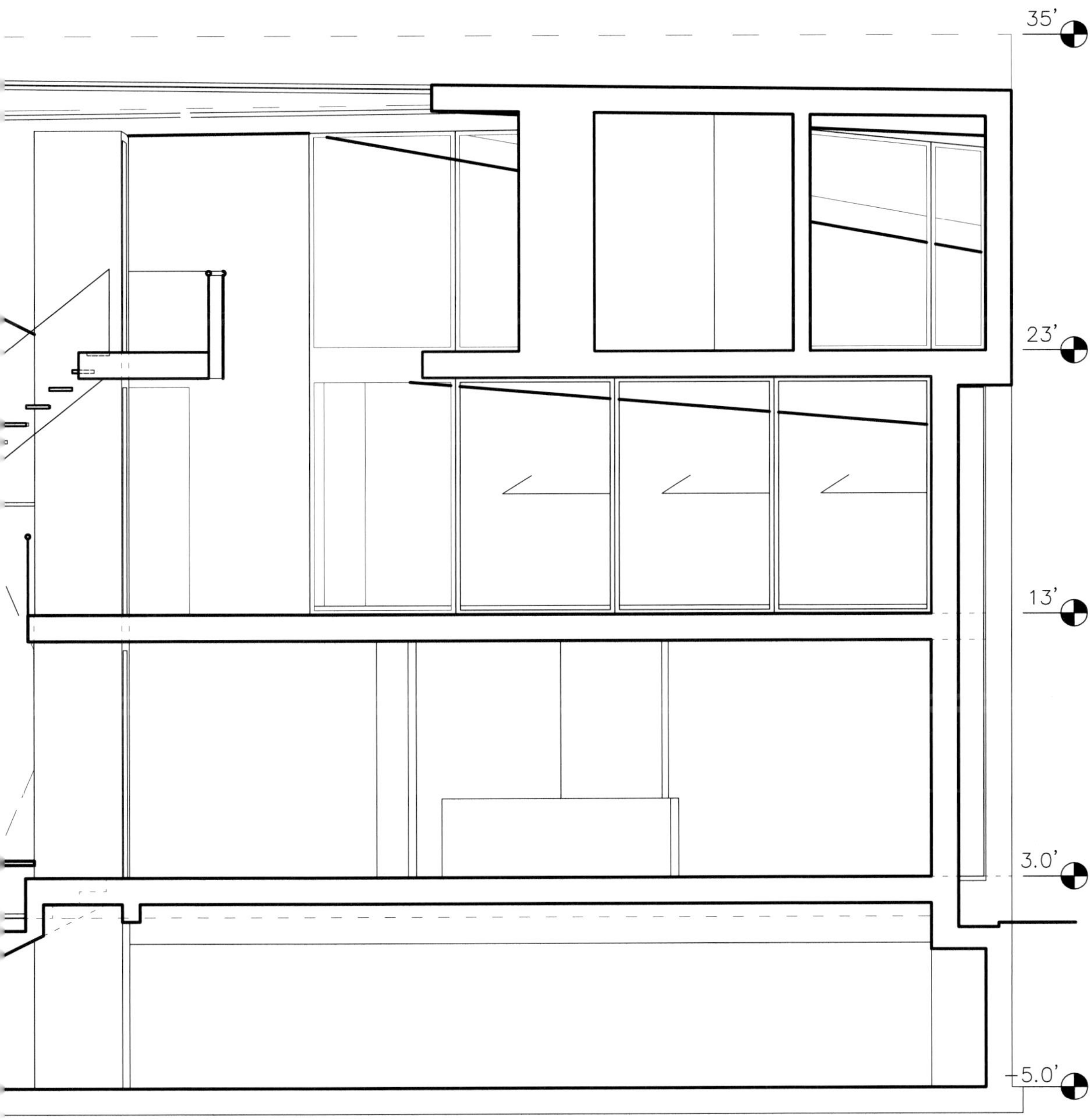
35’
23’
13’
3.0’
-5.0’

MODEL VIEWS

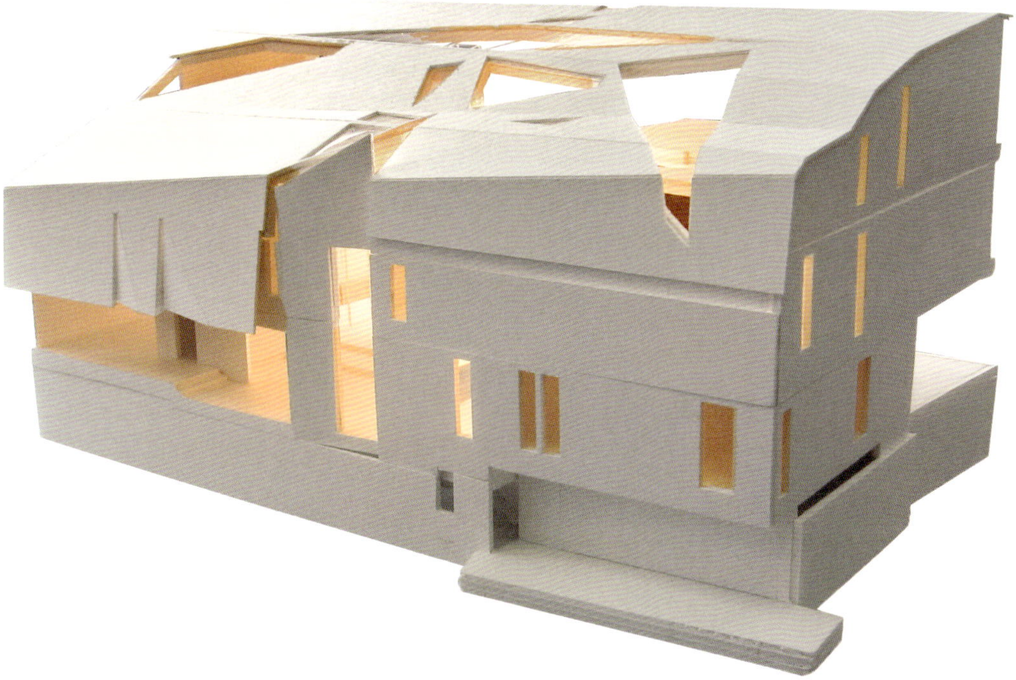

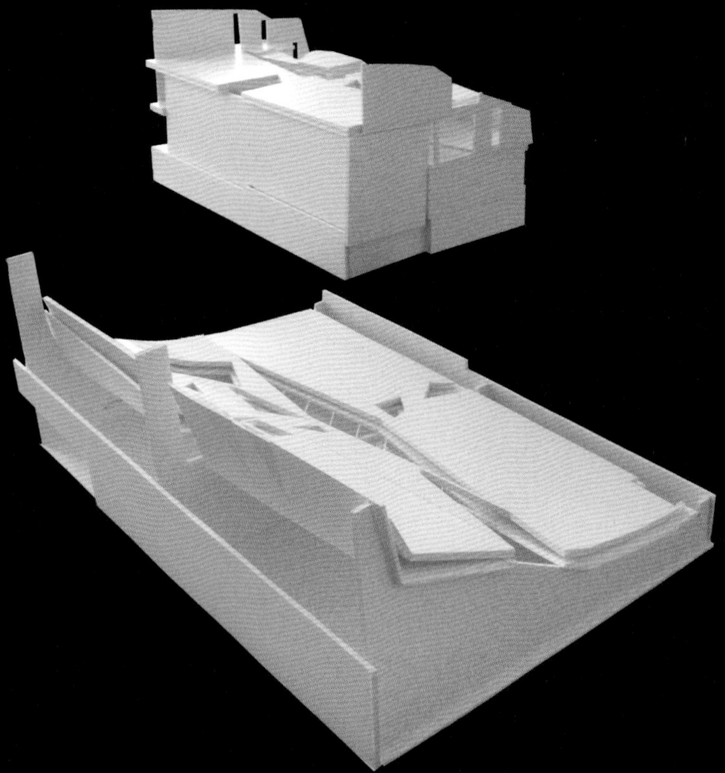

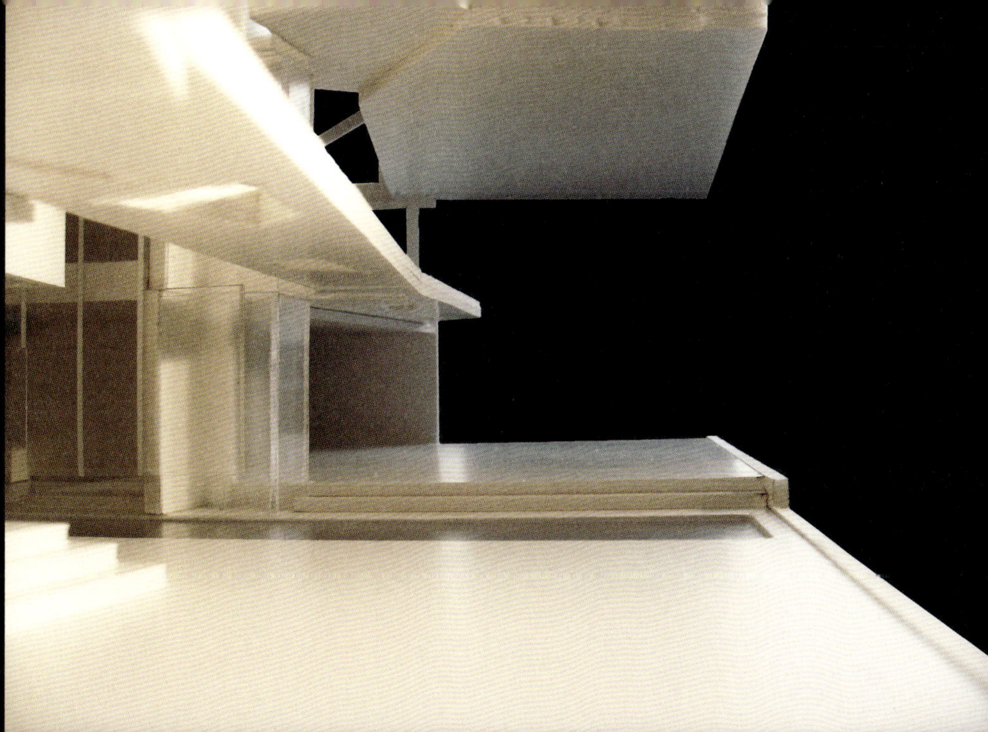

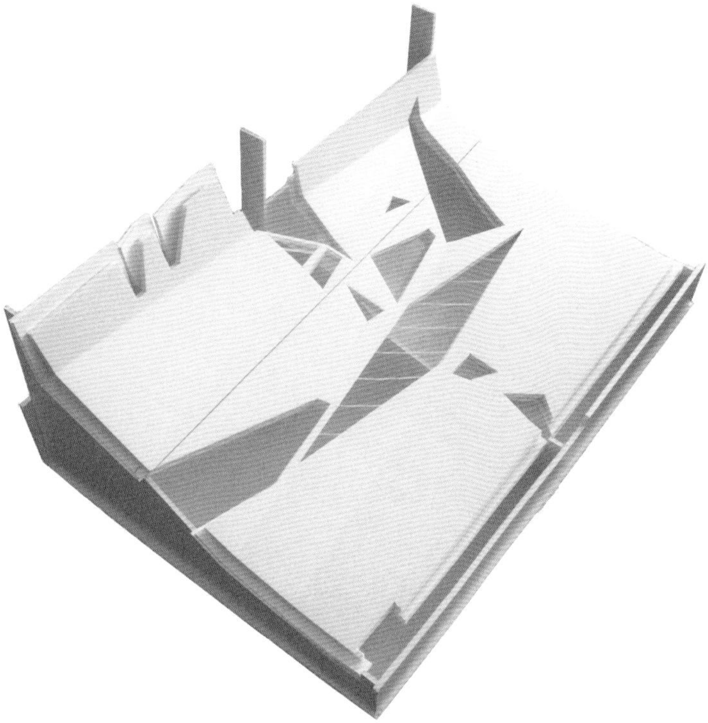

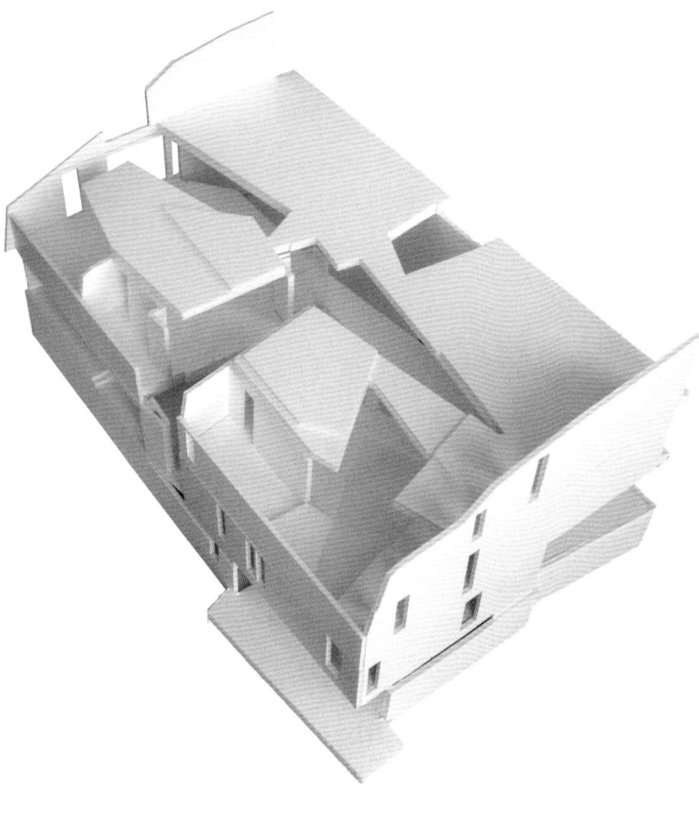

CONSTRUCTION

WORKING DRAWINGS

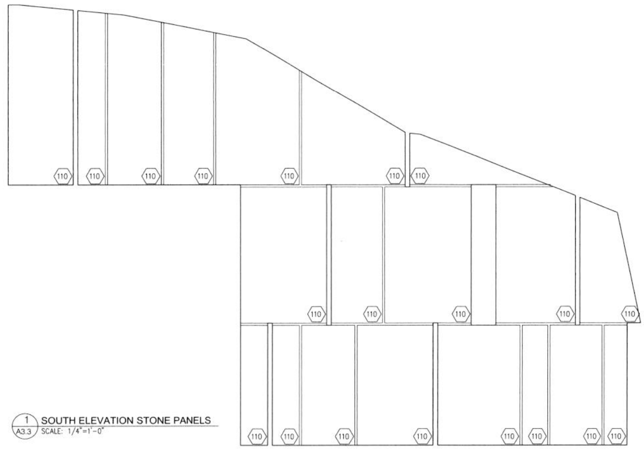

1 A3.3 SOUTH ELEVATION STONE PANELS
SCALE: 1/4"=1'-0"

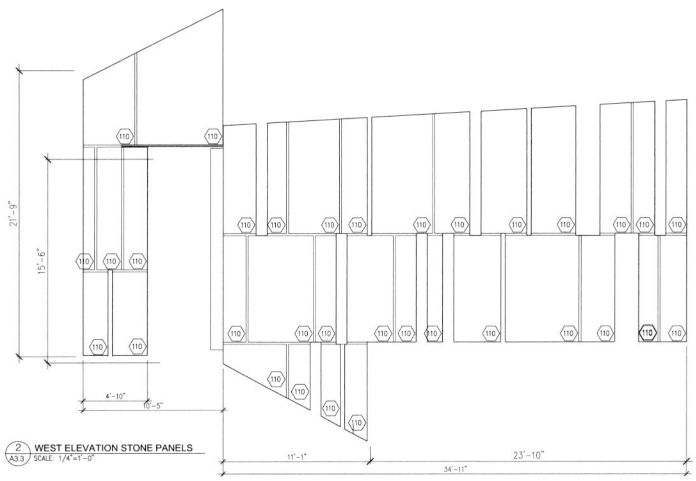

2 A3.3 WEST ELEVATION STONE PANELS
SCALE: 1/4"=1'-0"

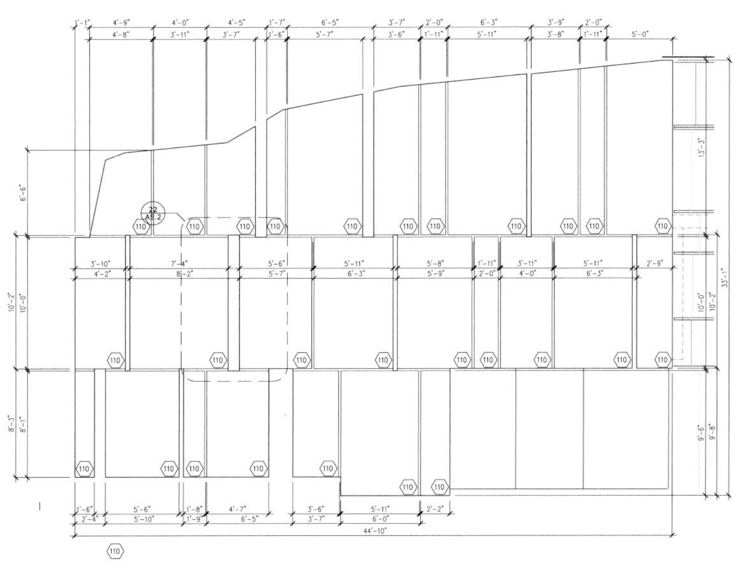

3 A3.3 NORTH ELEVATION STONE PANELS
SCALE: 1/4"=1'-0"

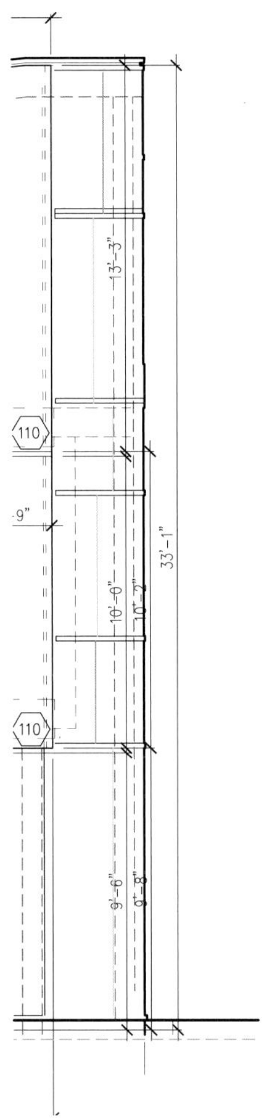

2 **SOUTH ELEVATION**
A3.0 SCALE: 3/16"=1'-0"

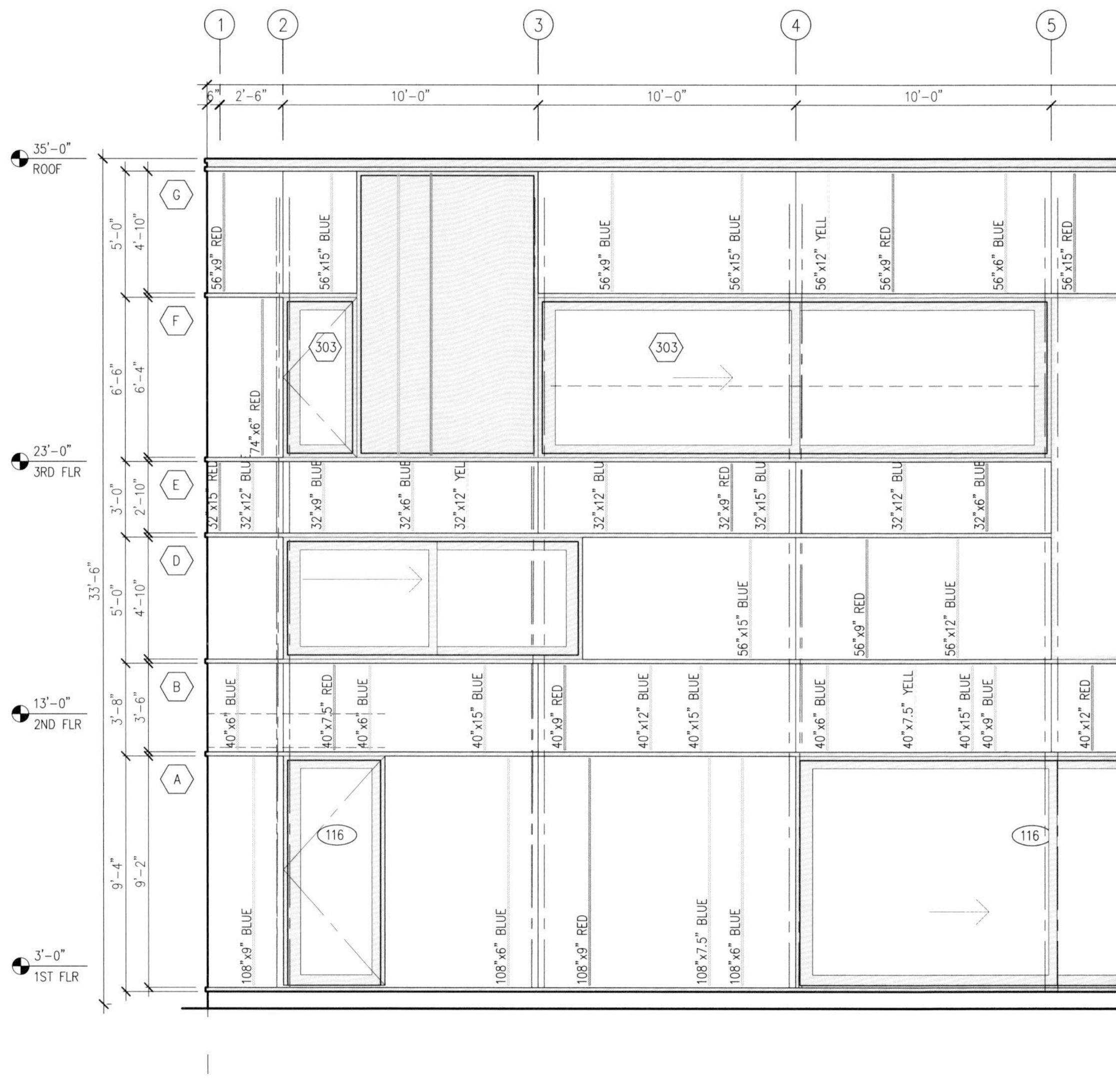

1 **EAST ELEVATION**
A3.0 SCALE: 3/16"=1'-0"

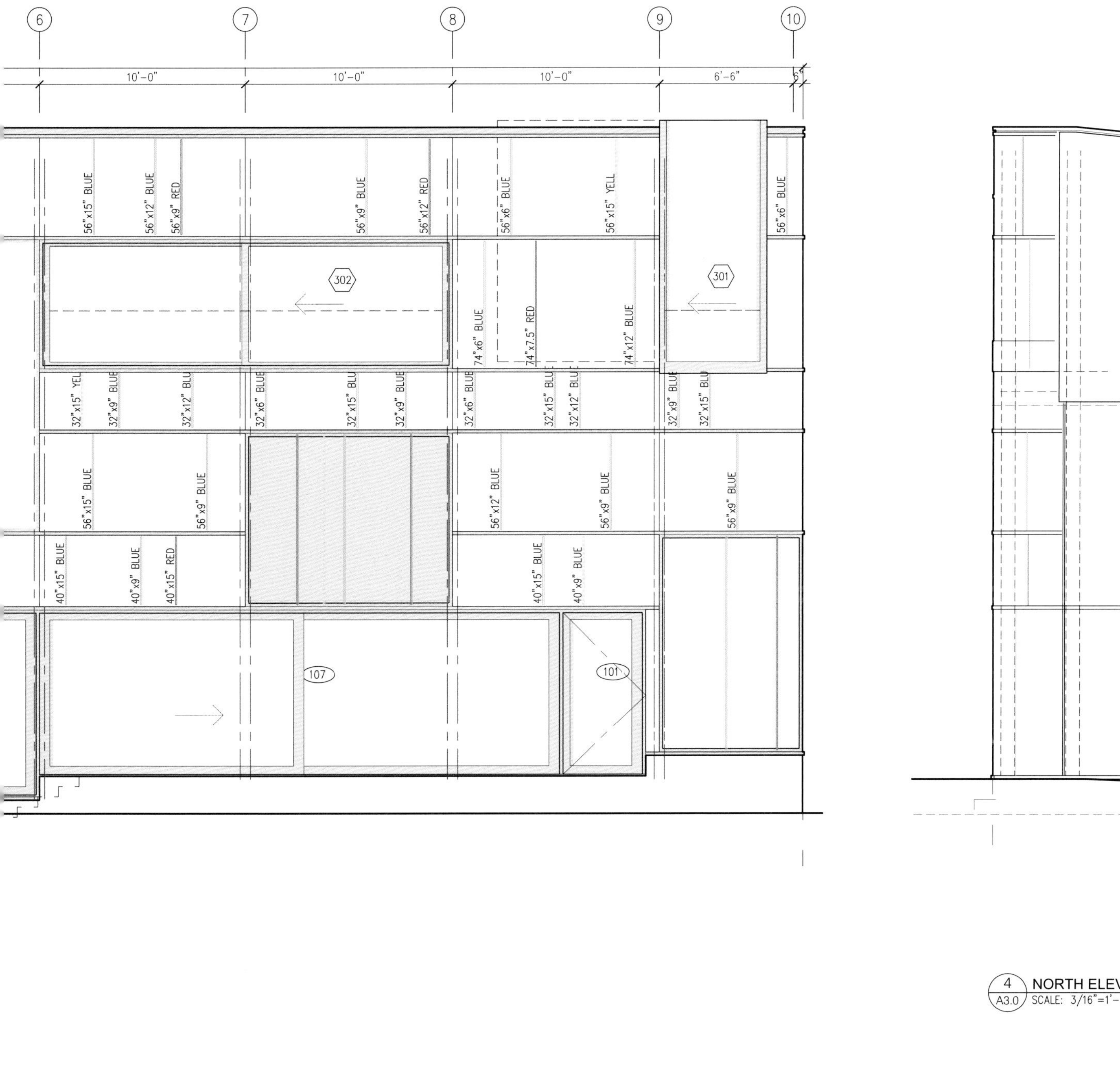

4 A3.0 NORTH ELEVATION
SCALE: 3/16"=1'-0"

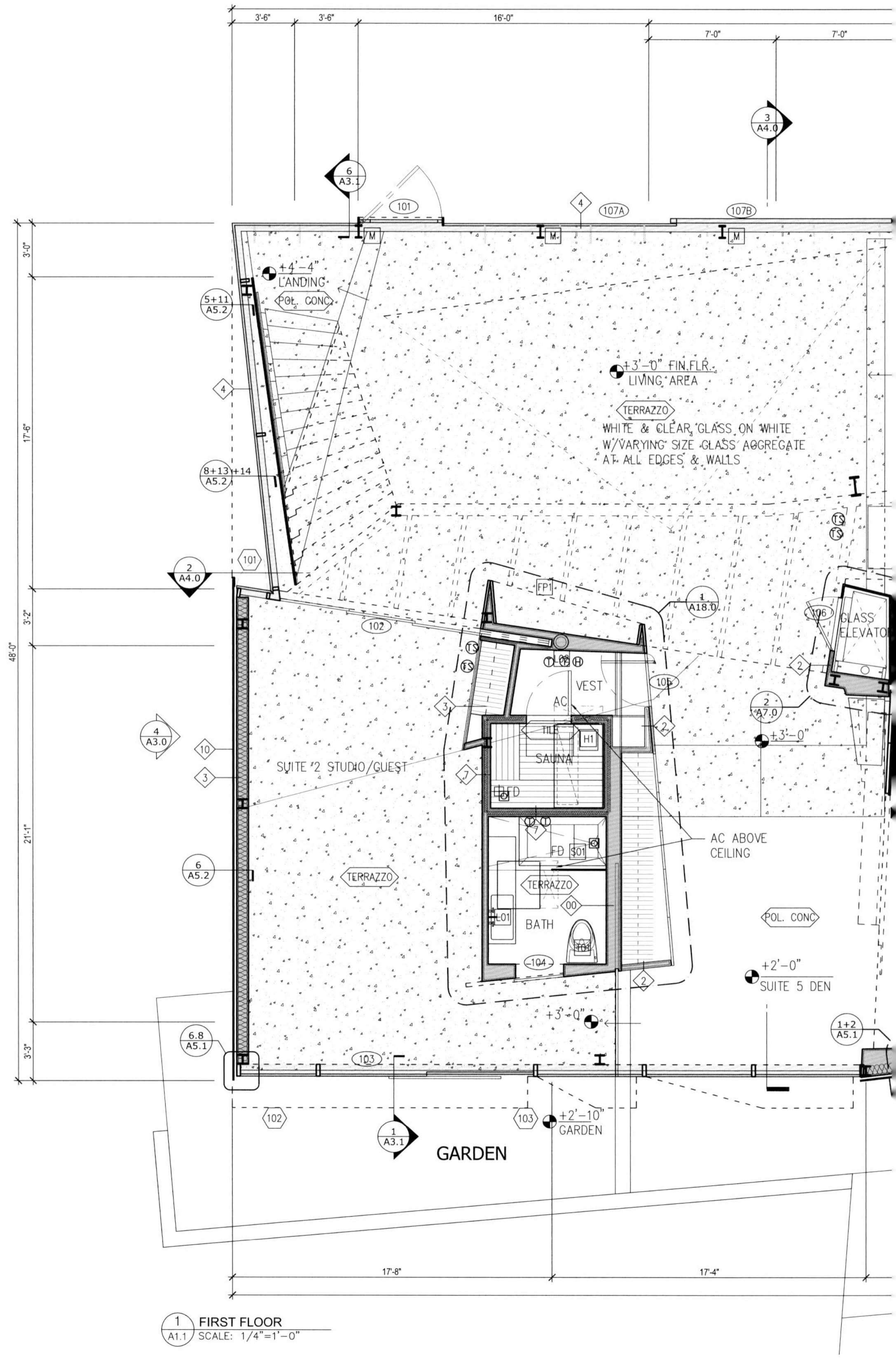
LANDING
LIVING AREA
TERRAZZO
WHITE & CLEAR GLASS ON WHITE
W/VARYING SIZE GLASS AGGREGATE
AT ALL EDGES & WALLS
SUITE 2 STUDIO/GUEST
VEST
SAUNA
BATH
AC ABOVE
CEILING
SUITE 5 DEN
GLASS
ELEVATOR
GARDEN
1 FIRST FLOOR
A1.1 SCALE: 1/4"=1'-0"

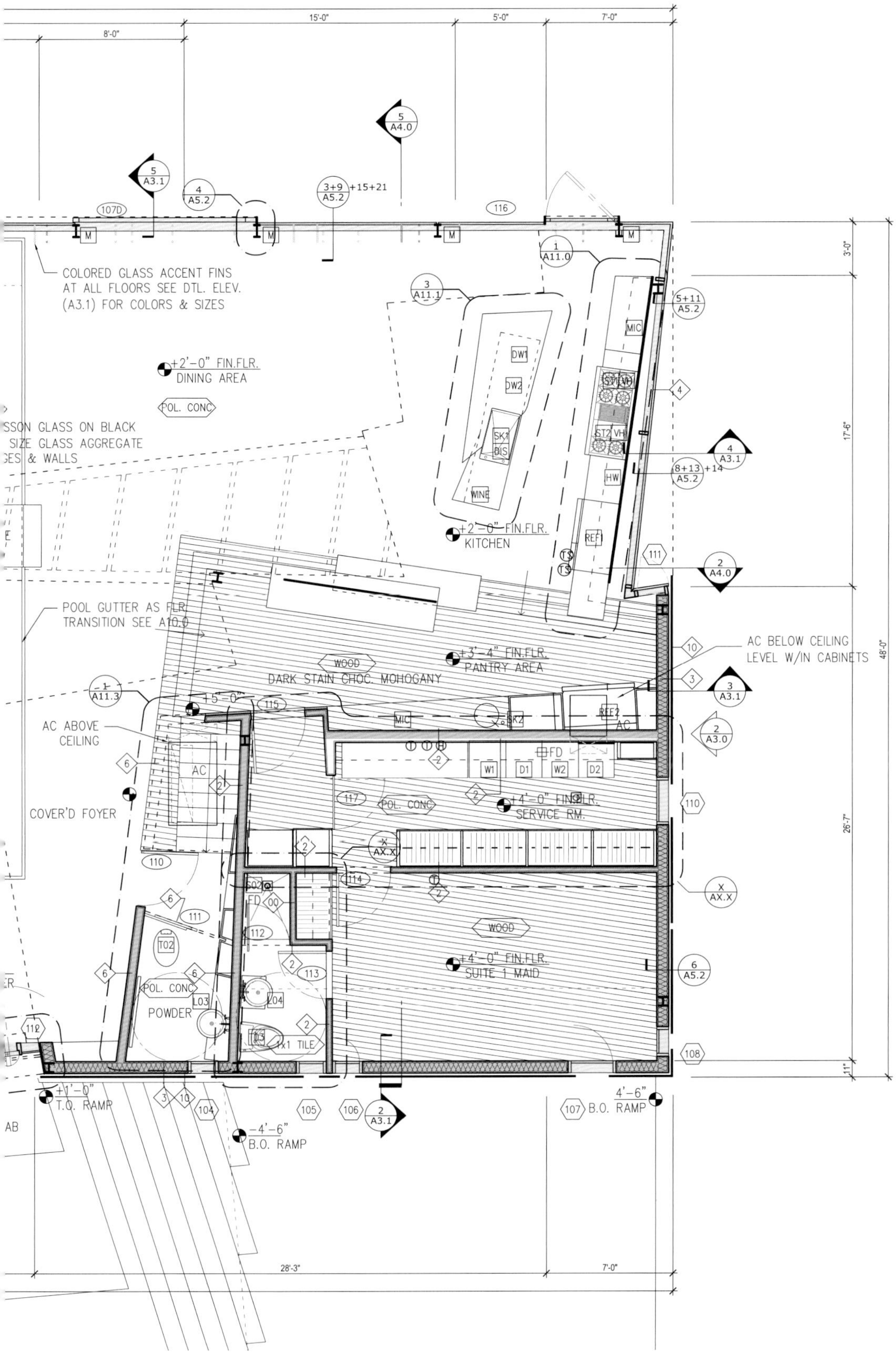

PARTITION LEGEND

SEE A6.0 FOR PARTITION SCHEDULE

- 0 — CONCRETE BEARING WALL OR RETAINING WALL
- 1 — INSULATED CONCRETE BEARING WALL OR RETAINING WALL
- 2 — INTERIOR MTL STUD WALL PARTITION W/ GYP BRD @ EACH SIDE
- 3 — EXTERIOR MTL STUD WALL PARTITION W/ GYP BRD ON INTERIOR & SHEATING ON EXTERIOR
- 4 — EXTERIOR DBL. GLASS CURTAIN WALL PARTITION
- 5 — FURR OUT PARTITION
- 6 — MILL WORK PARTITION OR MILL WORK
- 7 — SAUNA PARTITION
- 8 — FIRE PROOF PARTITION
- 9 — INTERIOR TEMPERED OR LAMINATED GLASS PARTITION
- 10 — EXTERIOR STONE RAINSCREEN

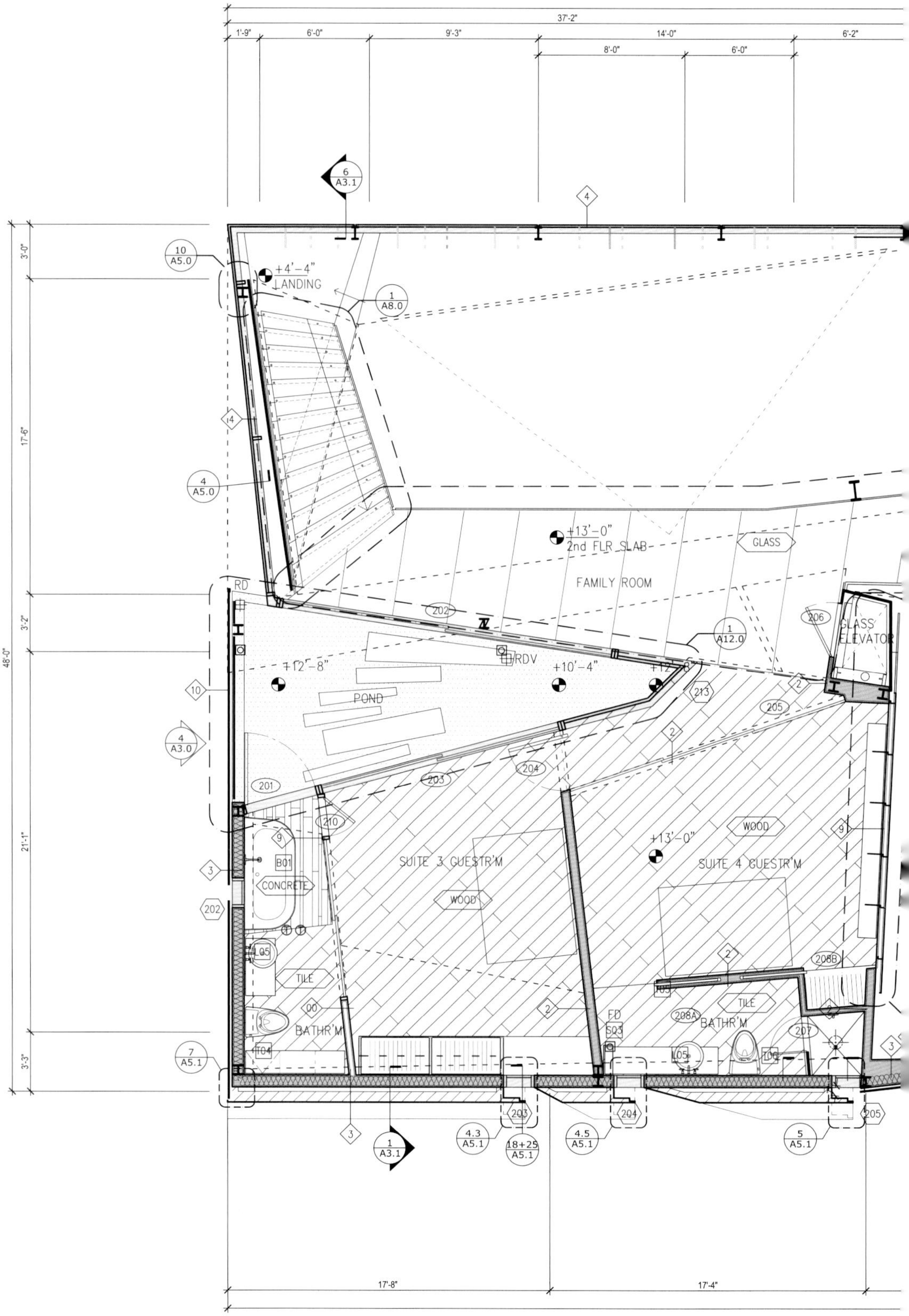

1 A1.2 SECOND FLOOR
SCALE: 1/4"=1'-0"

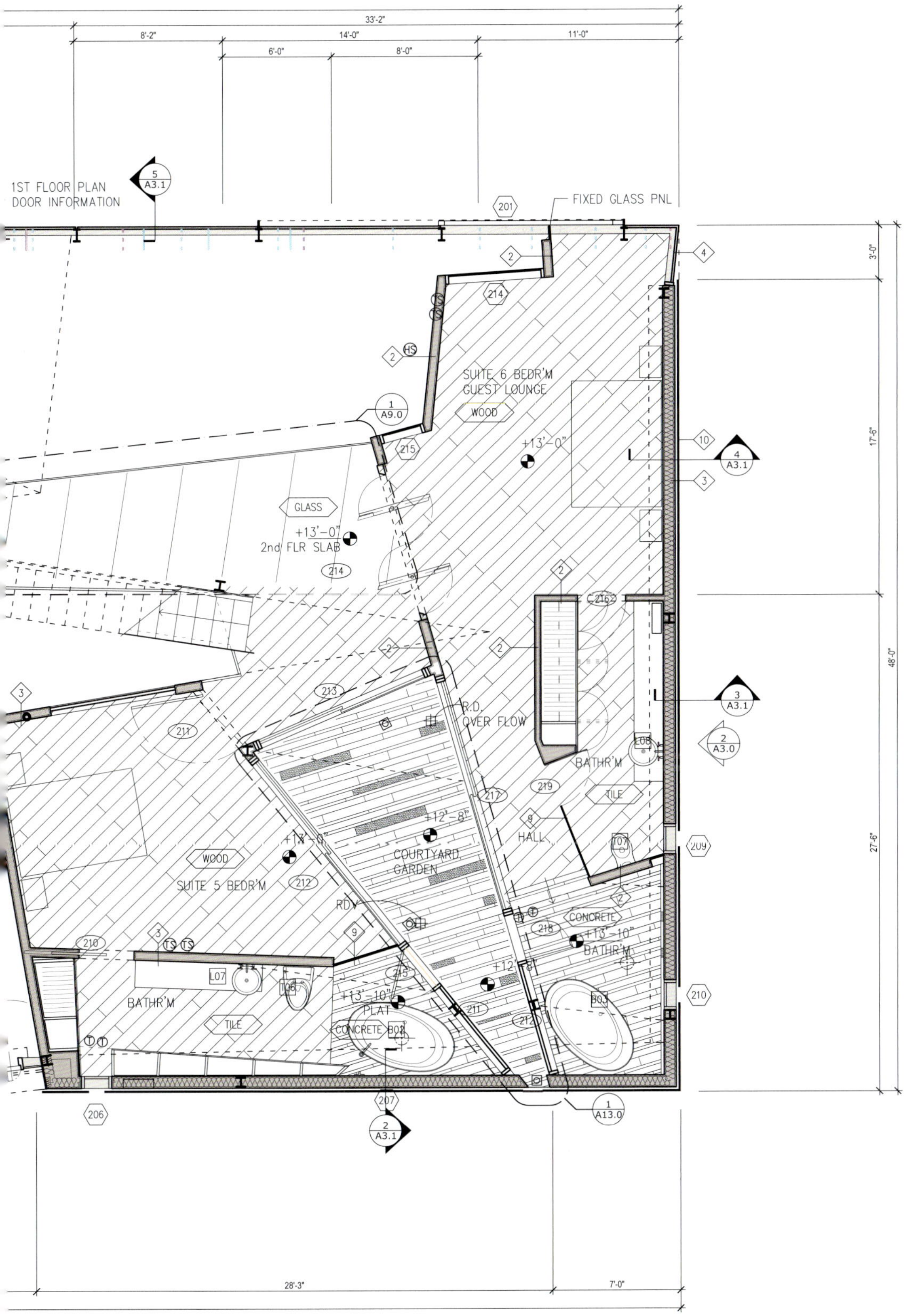

PARTITION LEGEND
SEE A6.0 FOR PARTITION SCHEDULE

- 0 — CONCRETE BEARING WALL OR RETAINING WALL
- 1 — INSULATED CONCRETE BEARING WALL OR RETAINING WALL
- 2 — INTERIOR MTL STUD WALL PARTITION W/ GYP BRD @ EACH SIDE
- 3 — EXTERIOR MTL STUD WALL PARTITION W/ GYP BRD ON INTERIOR & SHEATING ON EXTERIOR
- 4 — EXTERIOR DBL. GLASS CURTAIN WALL PARTITION
- 5 — FURR OUT PARTITION
- 6 — MILL WORK PARTITION OR MILL WORK
- 7 — SAUNA PARTITION
- 8 — FIRE PROOF PARTITION
- 9 — INTERIOR TEMPERED OR LAMINATED GLASS PARTITION
- 10 — EXTERIOR STONE RAINSCREEN

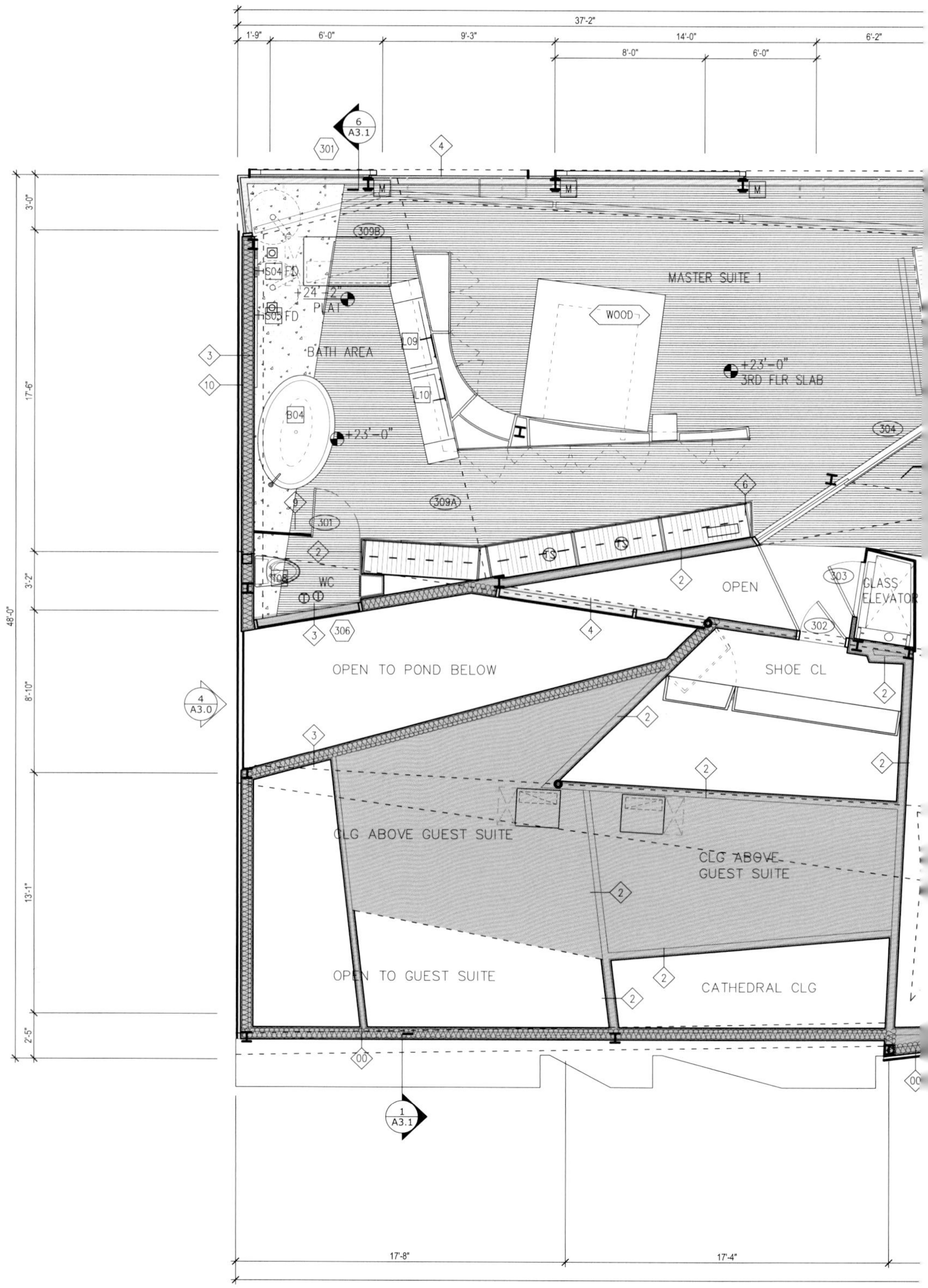

1 A1.3 THIRD FLOOR
SCALE: 1/4"=1'-0"

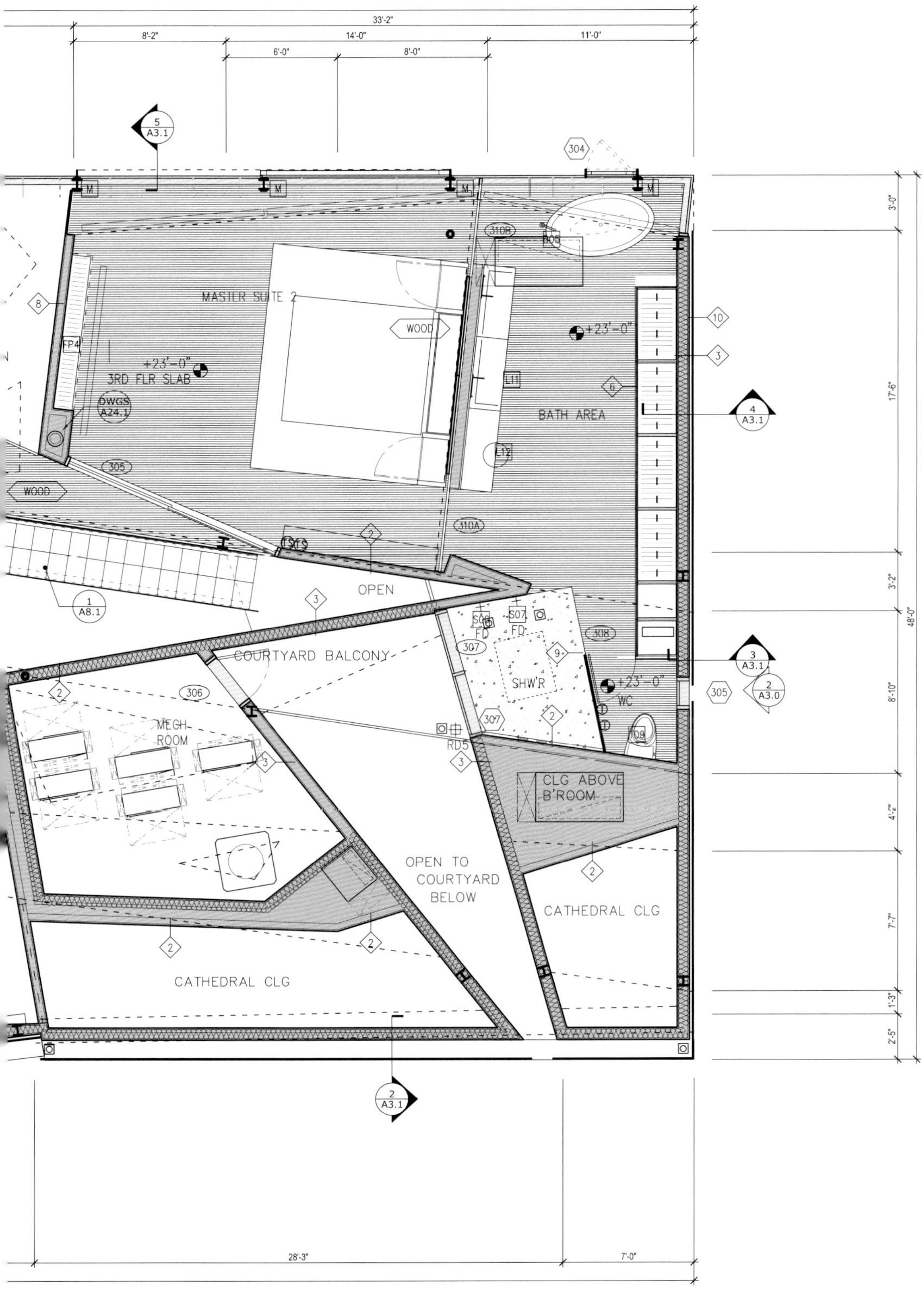

PARTITION LEGEND
SEE A6.0 FOR PARTITION SCHEDULE

- 0 — CONCRETE BEARING WALL OR RETAINING WALL
- 1 — INSULATED CONCRETE BEARING WALL OR RETAINING WALL
- 2 — INTERIOR MTL STUD WALL PARTITION W/ GYP BRD @ EACH SIDE
- 3 — EXTERIOR MTL STUD WALL PARTITION W/ GYP BRD ON INTERIOR & SHEATING ON EXTERIOR
- 4 — EXTERIOR DBL. GLASS CURTAIN WALL PARTITION
- 5 — FURR OUT PARTITION
- 6 — MILL WORK PARTITION OR MILL WORK
- 7 — SAUNA PARTITION
- 8 — FIRE PROOF PARTITION
- 9 — INTERIOR TEMPERED OR LAMINATED GLASS PARTITION
- 10 — EXTERIOR STONE RAINSCREEN

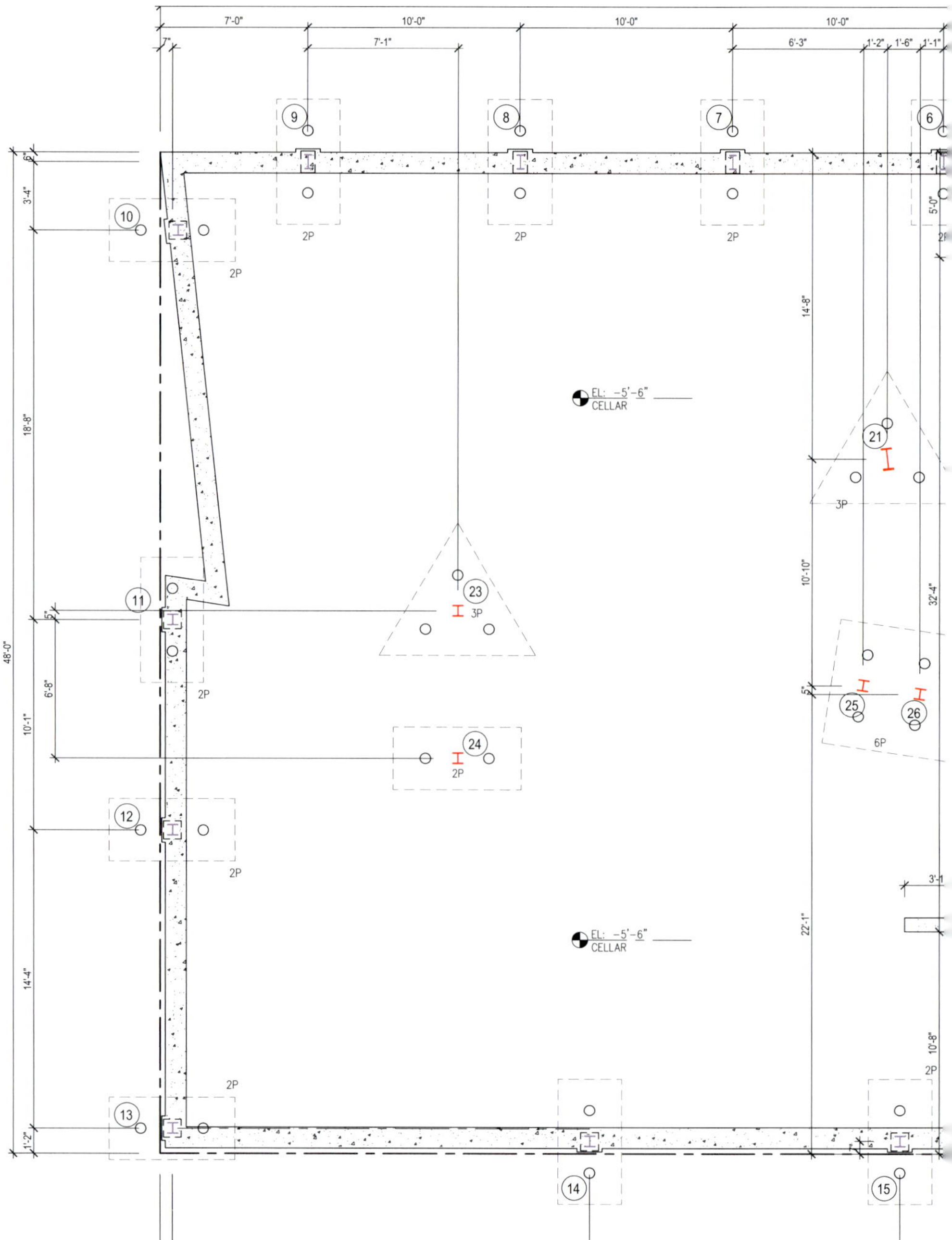

1 S1.0 CELLAR PLAN
SCALE 1/4"=1'-0"

COLUMN SCHEDULE AND SPECIAL NOTES:

1. ALL COLUMNS START AT FIRST FLOOR
2. TOP OF THE BASE PLATE IS 6" BELOW FIRST FLOOR ELEVATION SHOWN ON PLA/SECTIONS EITHER ON TOP OF EXTERIOR CONCRETE WALL OR INTERIOR 16"X16" CONCRETE PIERS.
3. ALL BASE PLATES ARE 3/4"X12X12 WITH ANCHOR BOLTS.
4. ALL COLUMNS ARE W 6X25.

COLS →	1 TO 9	10 TO 19	20/27	21	23	24	25/26
3RD FLR.	W6X25	W6X25	W6X25	—	W6X25	—	W6X25
2ND FLR.	W6X25	W6X25	W6X25	W6X25	W6X25	—	W6X25
1ST FLR.	W6X25	W6X25	W6X25	W6X25	W6X25	W6X25	W6X25
PIER CONC. ⊛	16X16 IN WALL	16X16 IN WALL	16X16	16X16	16X16	16X16	16X16
REINF. ⊛	4#7 #3	4#7 STIRRUPS	4#7 @ 12"	4#7	4#7	4#7	4#7
PILE GROUP	2P	2P	3P	3P	3P	2P	6P

⊛ || PROVIDE DOWELS INTO PILE CAP FOOTING FOR COLUMN PIERS AND EXTERIOR/SWIMMING POOL CONCRETE WALLS

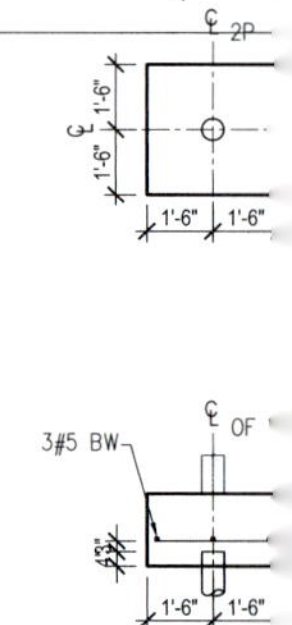

2 S1.0 1 PILE
SCALE: ¼

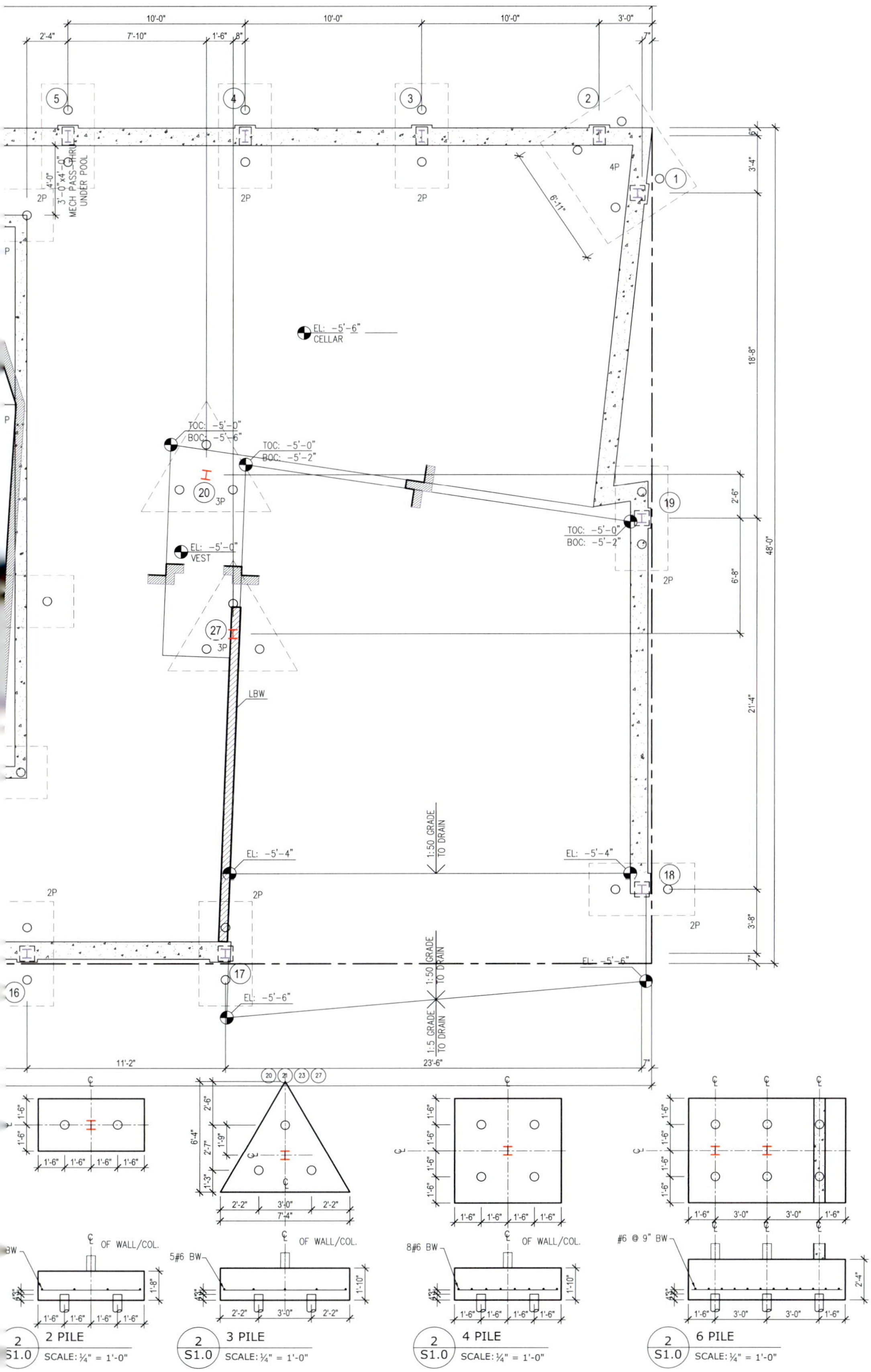
EL: -5'-6"
CELLAR
EL: -5'-0"
VEST
LBW
1:50 GRADE TO DRAIN
1:5 GRADE TO DRAIN
2 PILE
SCALE: 1/4" = 1'-0"
3 PILE
SCALE: 1/4" = 1'-0"
4 PILE
SCALE: 1/4" = 1'-0"
6 PILE
SCALE: 1/4" = 1'-0"

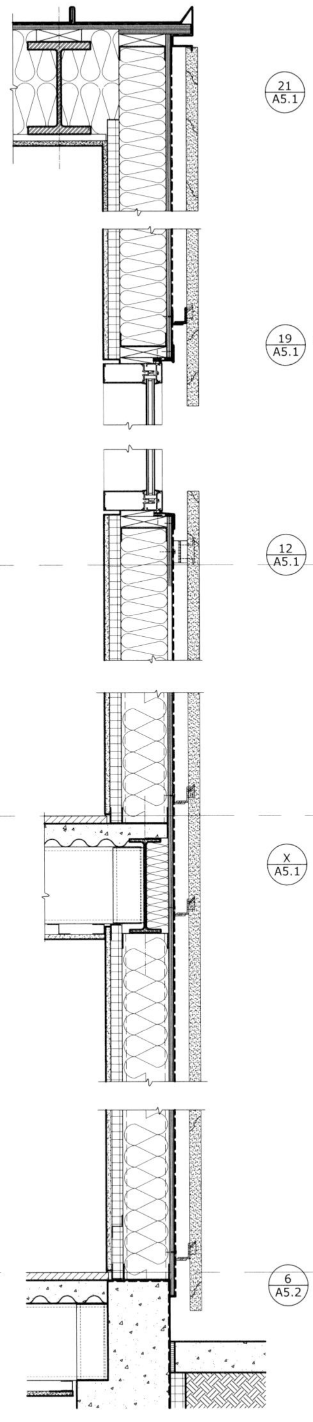

3 A3.1 CURTIAN WALL SECT DTL
SCALE: 1"=1'-0"

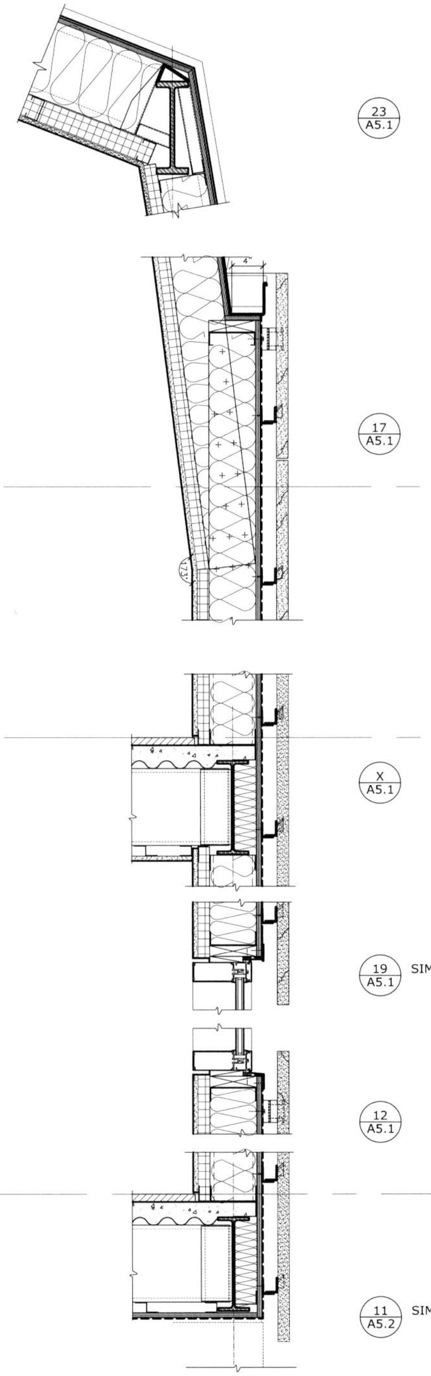

2 A3.1 CURTIAN WALL SECT DTL
SCALE: 1"=1'-0"

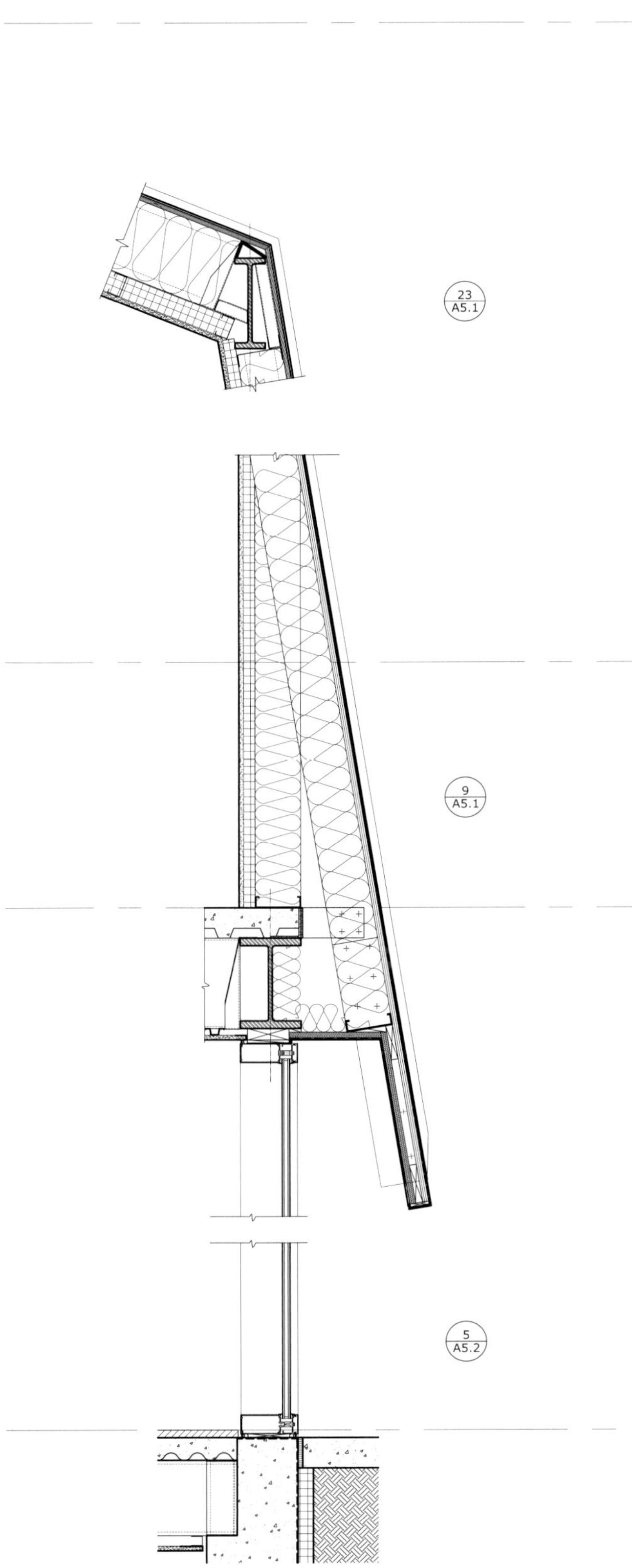

1 CURTIAN WALL SECT DTL
A3.1 SCALE: 1"=1'-0"

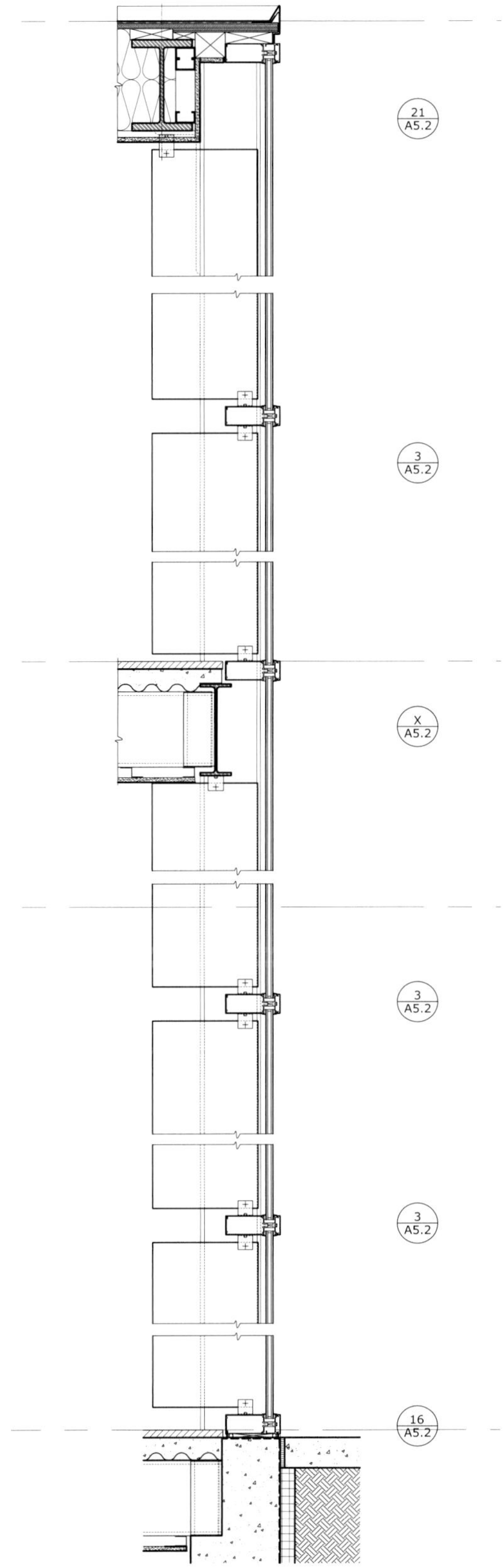

5 CURTIAN WALL SECT DTL
A3.1 SCALE: 1"=1'-0"

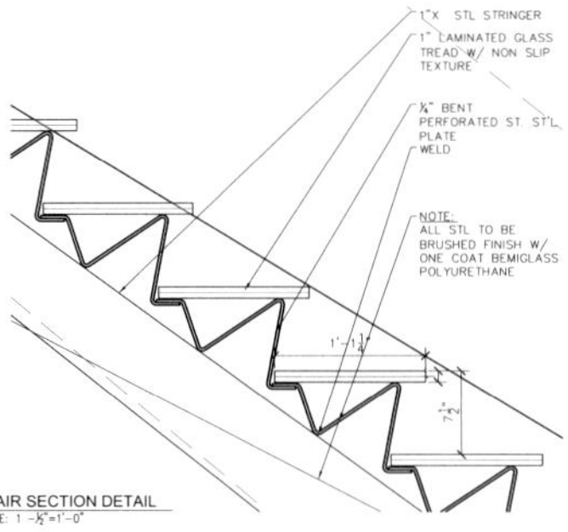

6 A8.0 STAIR SECTION DETAIL
SCALE: 1-½"=1'-0"

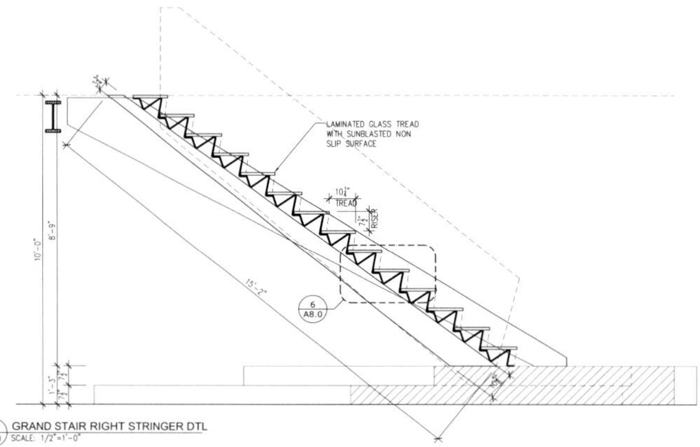

4 A8.0 GRAND STAIR RIGHT STRINGER DTL
SCALE: 1/2"=1'-0"

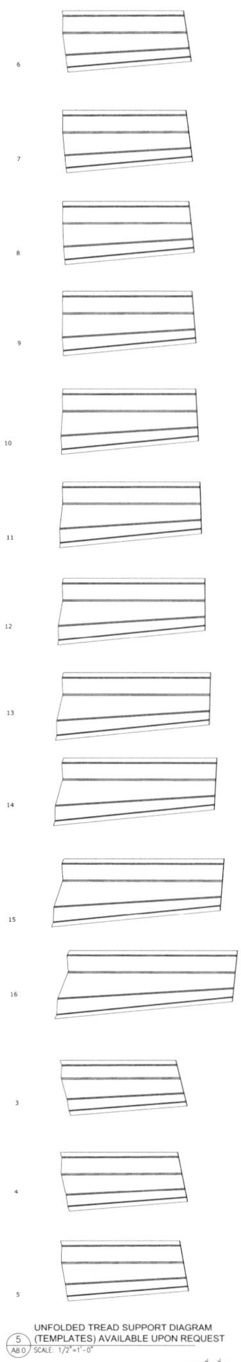

5 A8.0 UNFOLDED TREAD SUPPORT DIAGRAM (TEMPLATES) AVAILABLE UPON REQUEST
SCALE: 1/2"=1'-0"

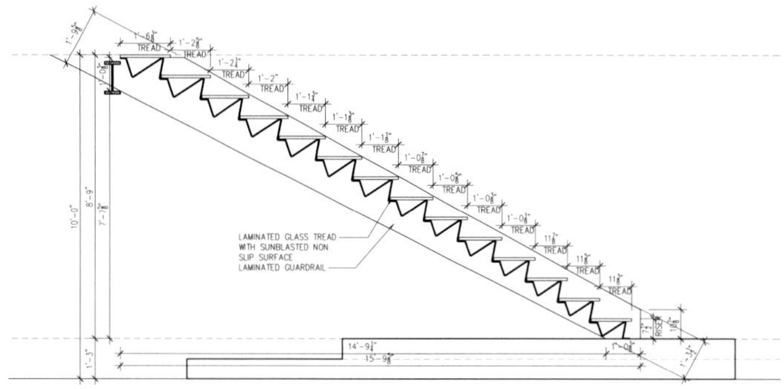

3 A8.0 GRAND STAIR LEFT STRINGER DTL
SCALE: 1/2"=1'-0"

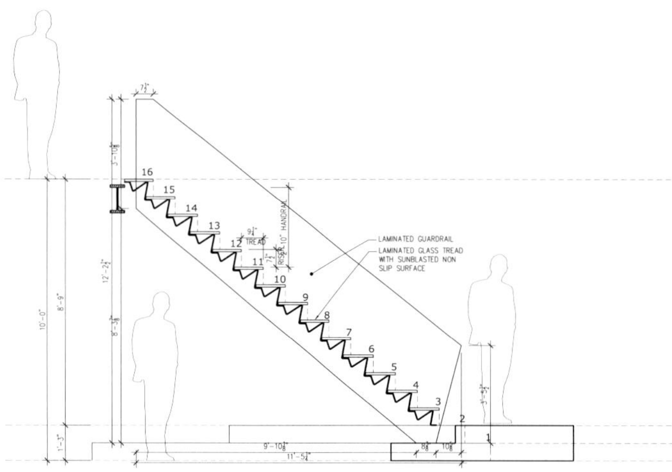

2 A8.0 GRAND STAIR SECTION
SCALE: 1/2"=1'-0"

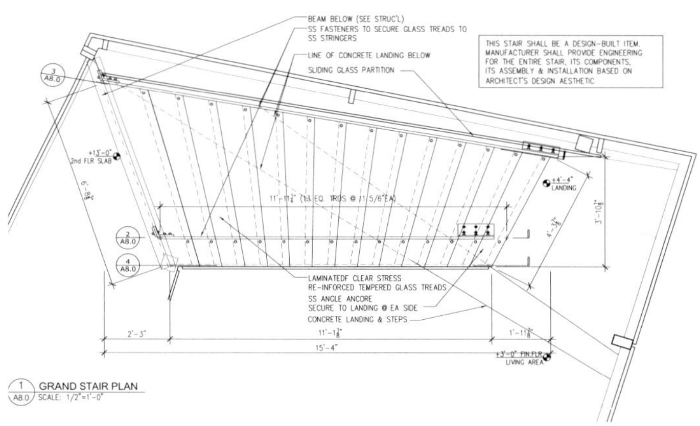

1 A8.0 GRAND STAIR PLAN
SCALE: 1/2"=1'-0"

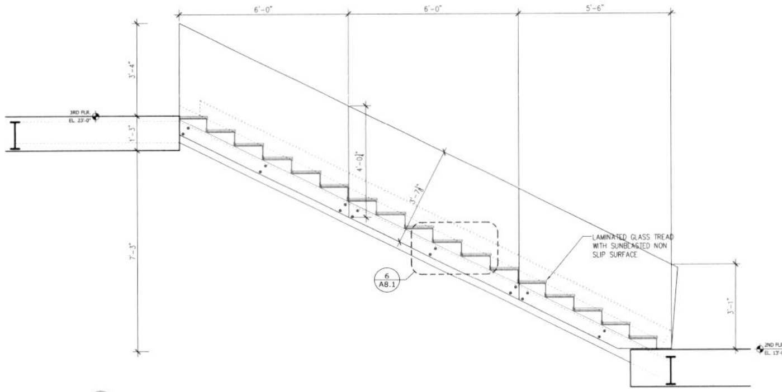

3 A8.1 STAIR ELEVATION 1
SCALE: 1/2"=1'-0"

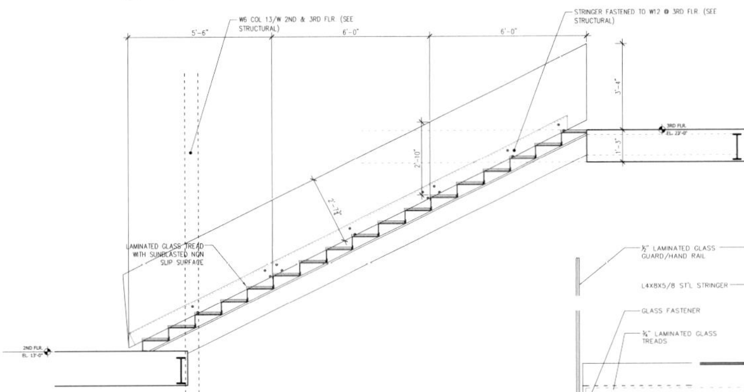

4 A8.1 STAIR ELEVATION 2
SCALE: 1/2"=1'-0"

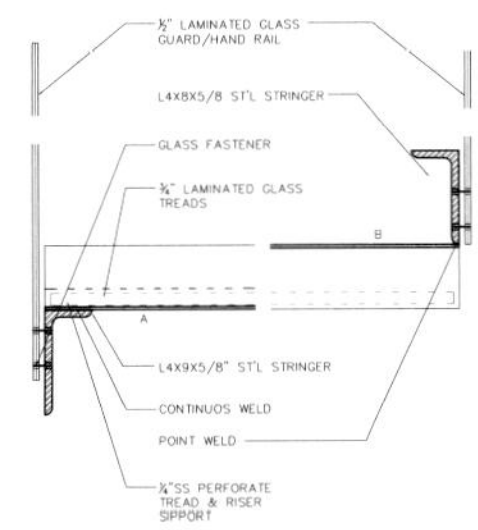

5 A8.1 STAIR CROOS DETAIL SECTION
SCALE: 1-1/2"=1'-0"

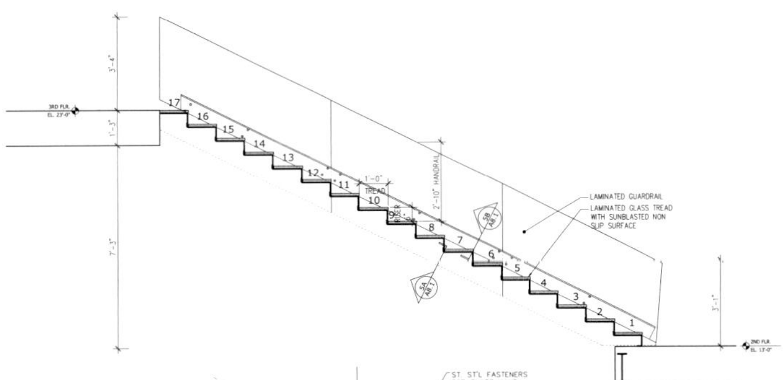

2 A8.1 STAIR SECTION 1
SCALE: 1/2"=1'-0"

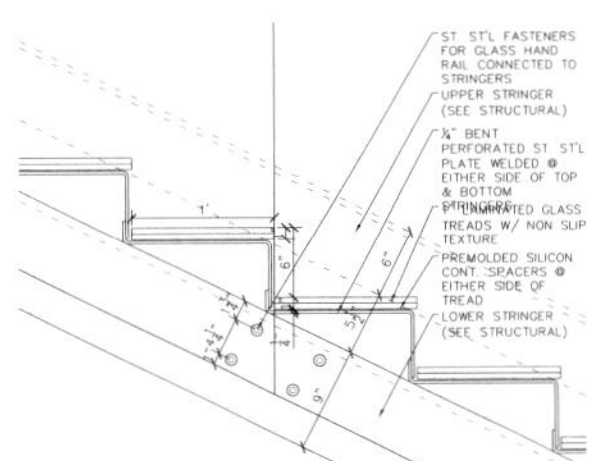

THIS STAIR SHALL BE A DESIGN-BUILT ITEM. MANUFACTURER SHALL PROVIDE ENGINEERING FOR THE ENTIRE STAIR, ITS COMPONENTS, ITS ASSEMBLY & INSTALLATION BASED ON ARCHITECT'S DESIGN AESTHETIC

6 A8.1 STAIR SECTION DETAIL
SCALE: 1-½"=1'-0"

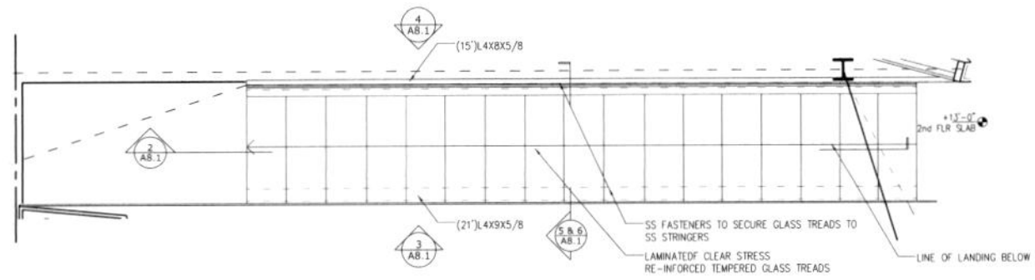

1 A8.1 STAIR PLAN
SCALE: 1/2"=1'-0"

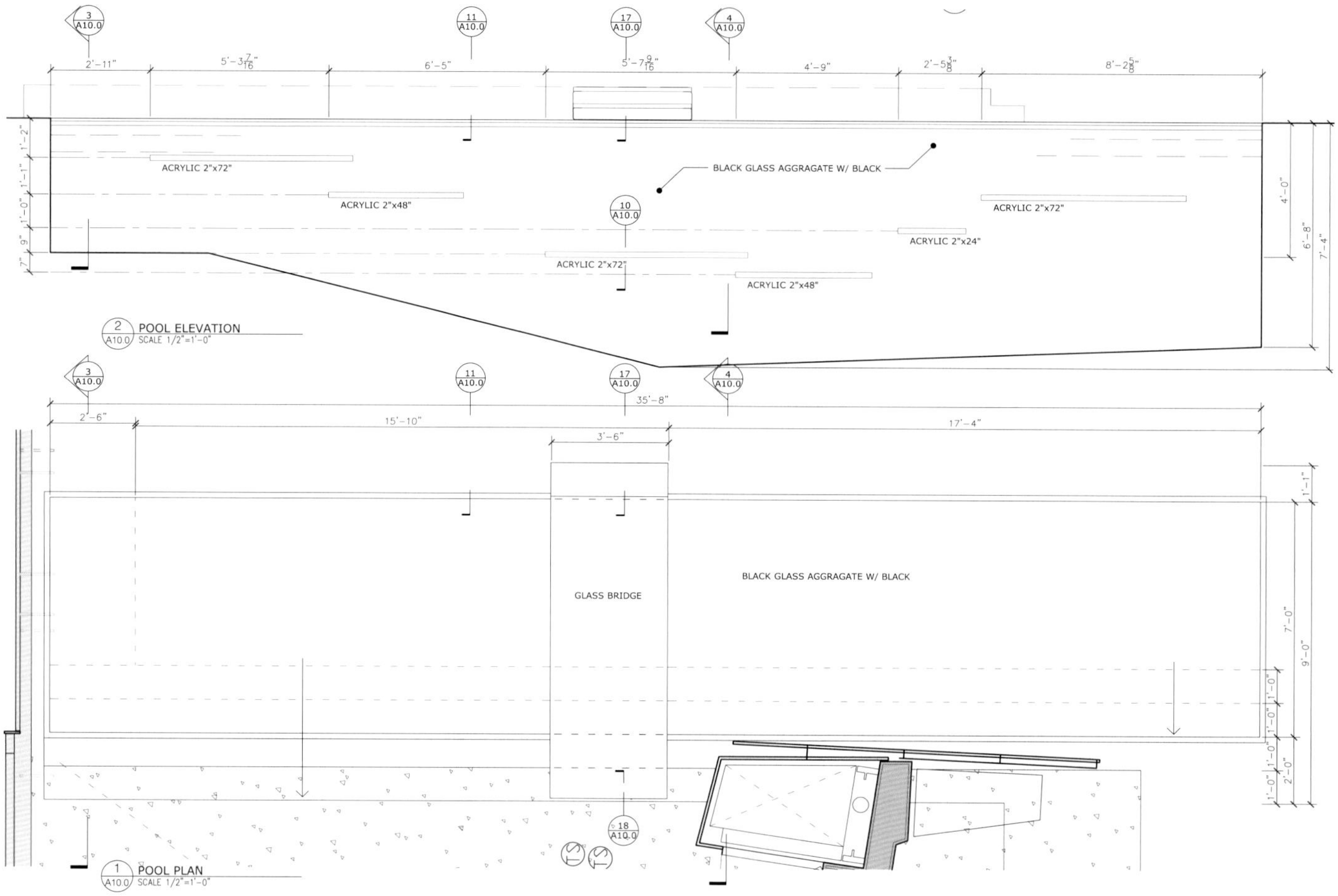

2 POOL ELEVATION
SCALE 1/2"=1'-0"
ACRYLIC 2"x72"
ACRYLIC 2"x48"
BLACK GLASS AGGRAGATE W/ BLACK
ACRYLIC 2"x72"
ACRYLIC 2"x24"
ACRYLIC 2"x48"
1 POOL PLAN
SCALE 1/2"=1'-0"
GLASS BRIDGE
BLACK GLASS AGGRAGATE W/ BLACK
35'-8"
15'-10"
17'-4"
3'-6"

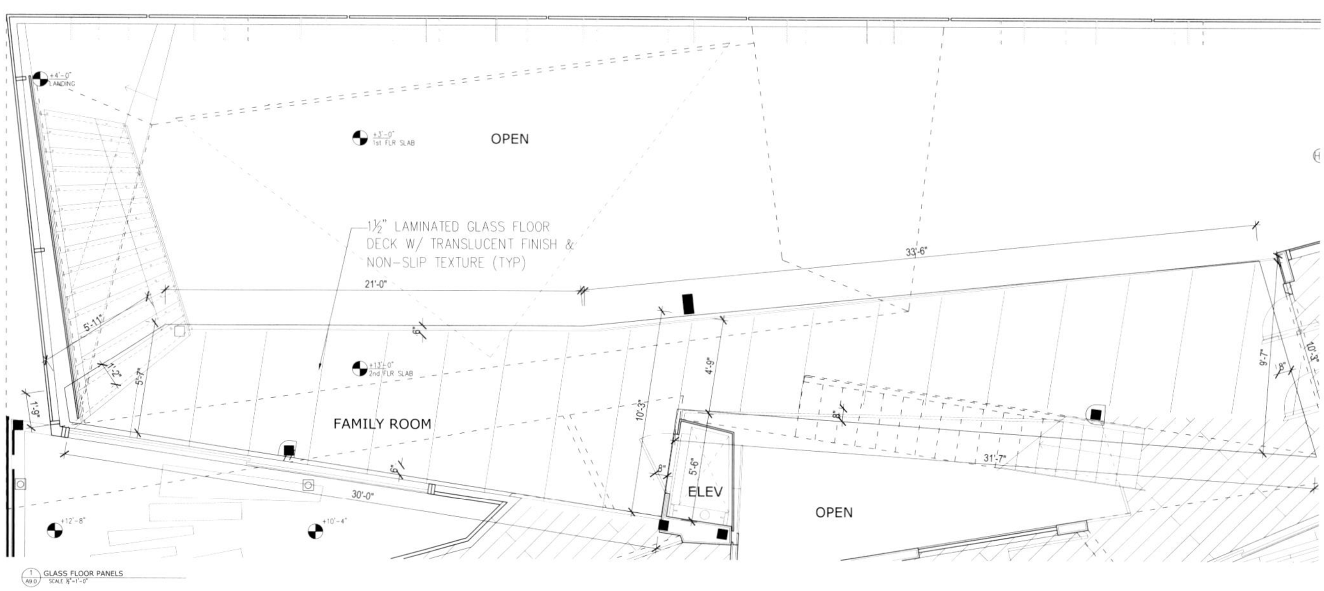

OPEN
1½" LAMINATED GLASS FLOOR
DECK W/ TRANSLUCENT FINISH &
NON-SLIP TEXTURE (TYP)
FAMILY ROOM
ELEV
OPEN
1 GLASS FLOOR PANELS

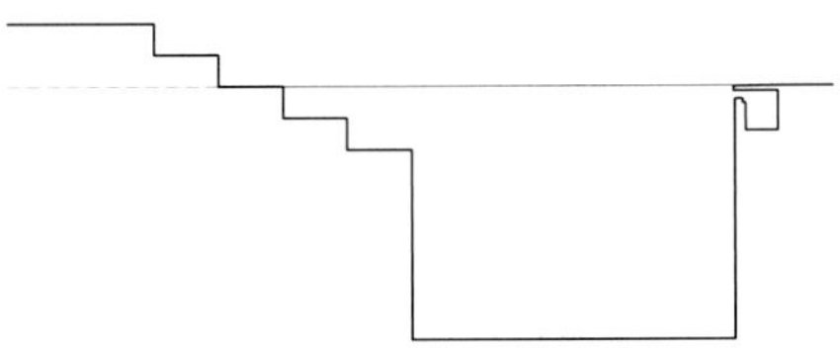

3 A10.0 POOL CROSS SECTION @ SHALLOW
SCALE 1/2"=1'-0"

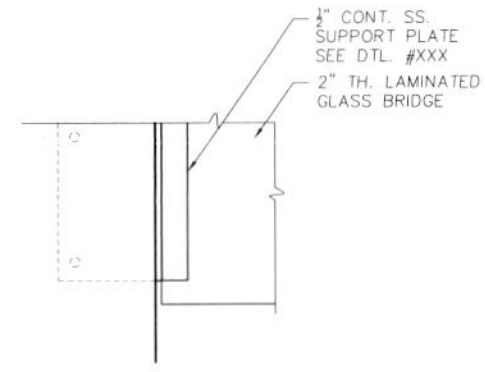

25 A10.0 GLASS BRIDGE SUPPORT DTL.
SCALE: 1½"=1'-0"

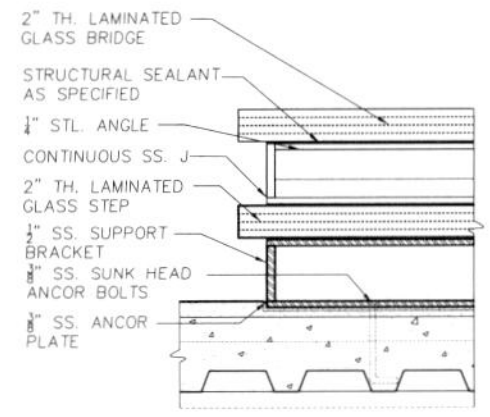

24 A10.0 POOL ELEV. DTL.
SCALE: 1½"=1'-0"

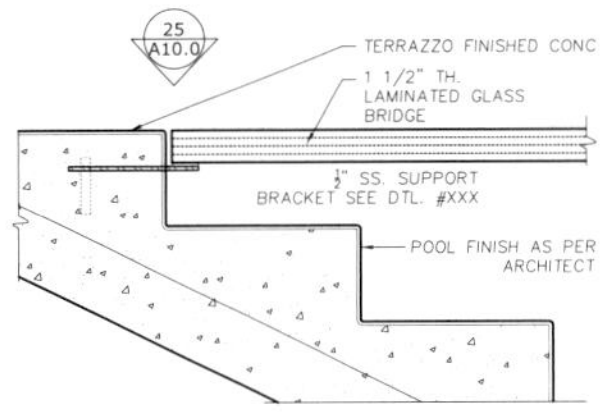

18 A10.0 POOL DTL.
SCALE: 1½"=1'-0"

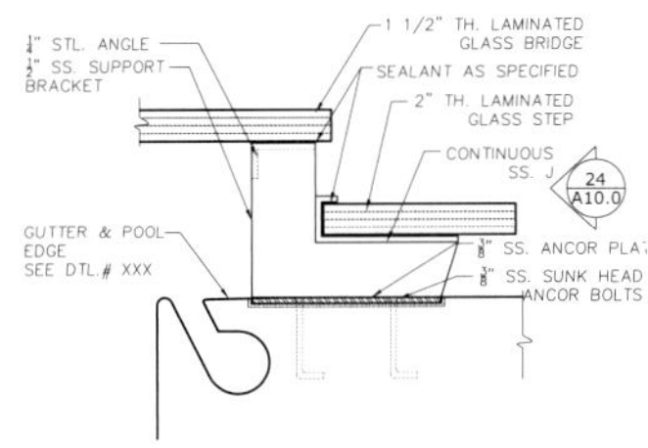

17 A10.0 POOL BRIDGE STAIR DTL.
SCALE: 1½"=1'-0"

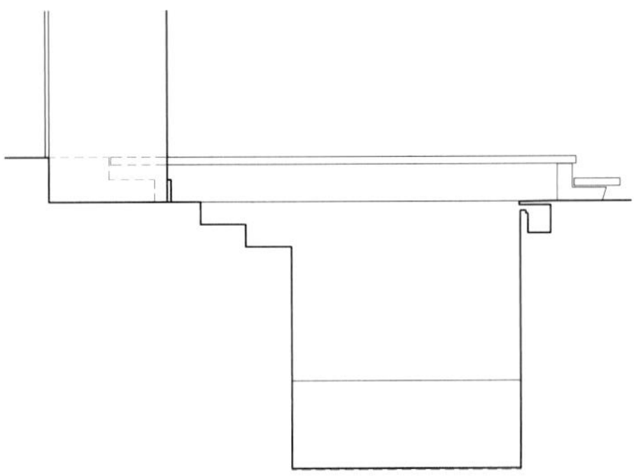

4 A10.0 POOL CROSS SECTION @ CTR
SCALE 1/2"=1'-0"

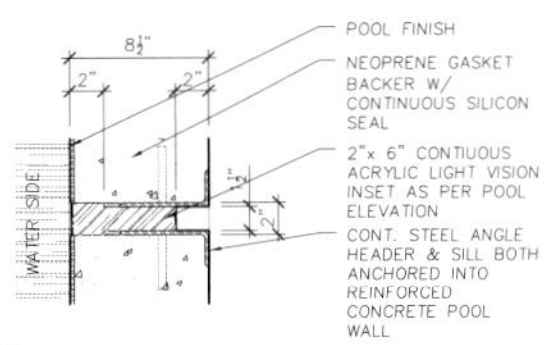

11 A10.0 POOL LIGHT DTL.
SCALE: 1½"=1'-0"

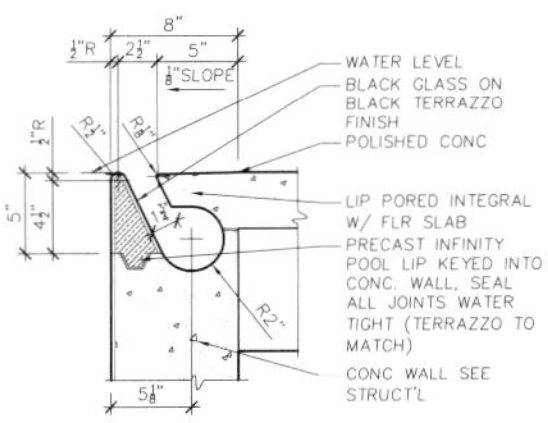

10 A5.0 POOL GUTTER DTL.
SCALE: 1½"=1' 0"

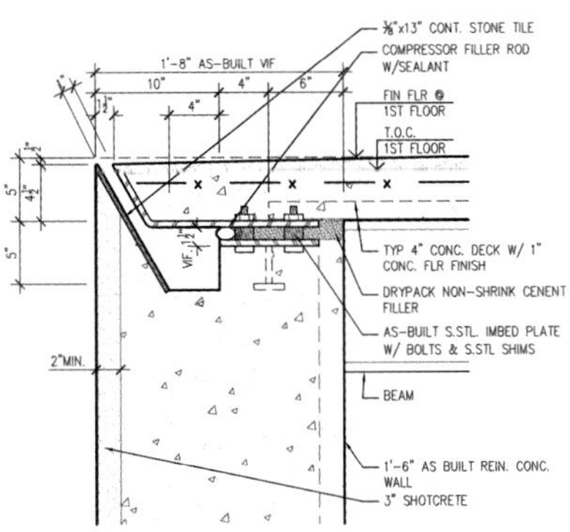

6A SK POOLEDGE @ IMBED PL
SCALE 1½"=1'-0"
SIM DTL: 5/S4.4
FOR REVIEW SEPT 4TH 2009

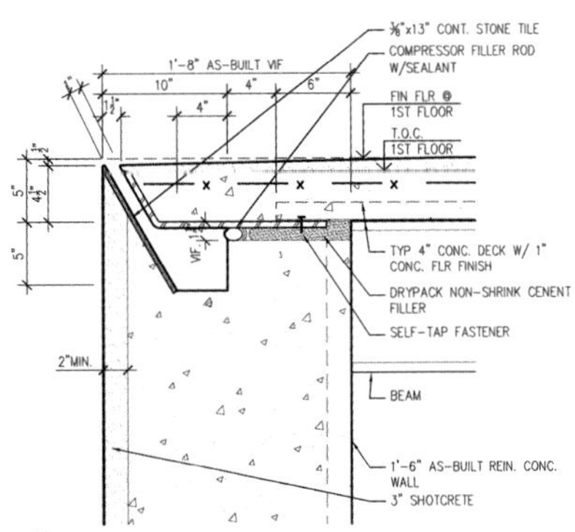

6B SK POOL EDGE B/W IMBED PL
SCALE 1½"=1'-0"
SIM DTL: 5/S4.4
FOR REVIEW SEPT 4TH 2009

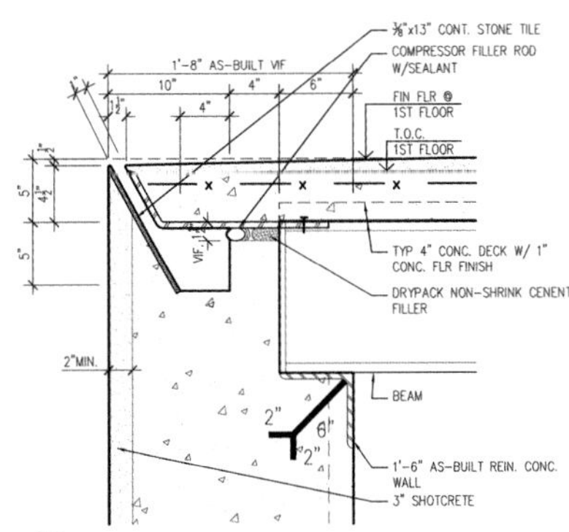

6C SK POOL EDGE @ BM PCKT
SCALE 1½"=1'-0"
SIM DTL: 5/S4.4
FOR REVIEW SEPT 4TH 2009

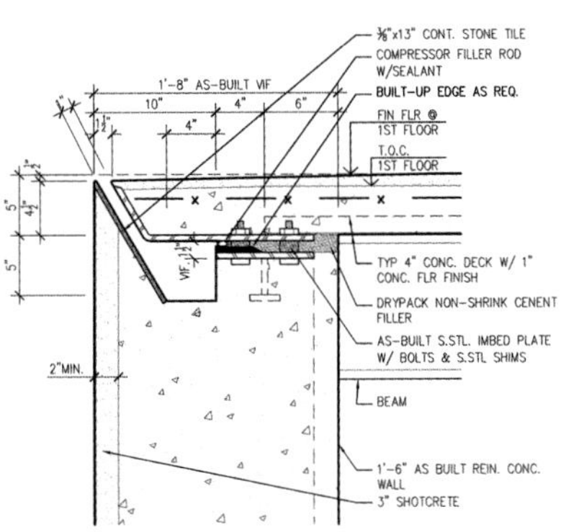

6A SK POOLEDGE @ IMBED PL - ALTERNATE I
SCALE 1½"=1'-0"
FOR REVIEW SEPT 4TH 2009

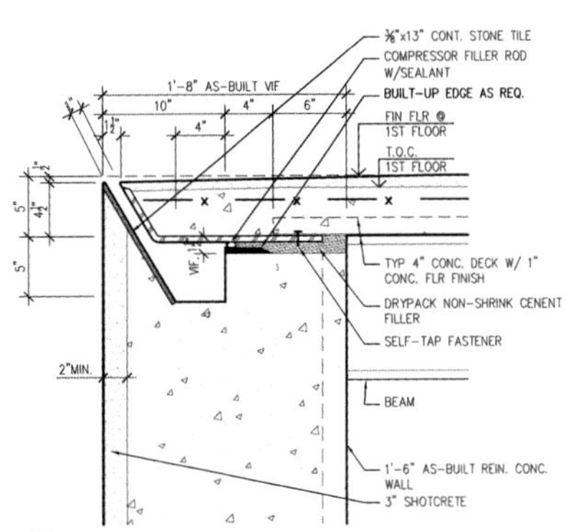

6B SK POOL EDGE B/W IMBED PL - ALTERNATE I
SCALE 1½"=1'-0"
FOR REVIEW SEPT 4TH 2009

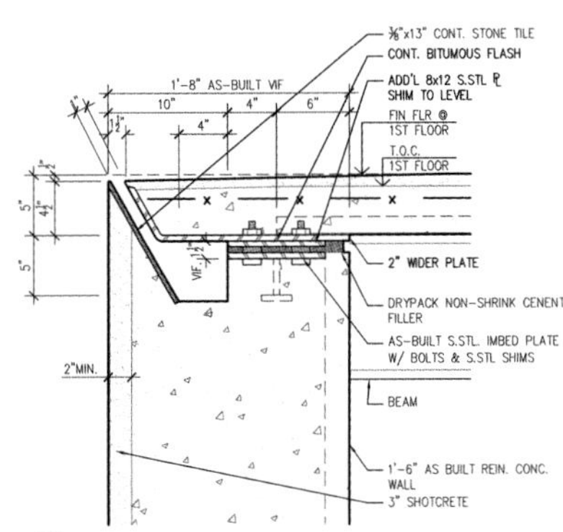

6A SK POOLEDGE @ IMBED PL - ALTERNATE II
SCALE 1½"=1'-0"
FOR REVIEW SEPT 4TH 2009

PROCESS

BOSTITCH

THE BUILDING

KOONS

KOONS

KOONS

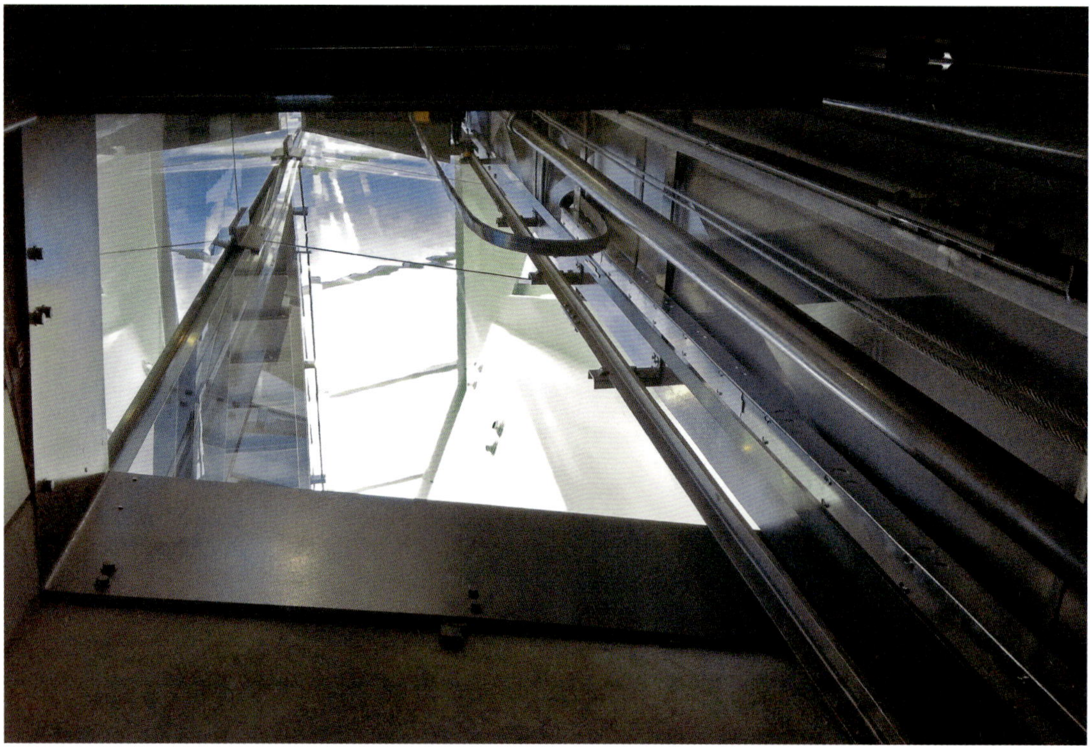

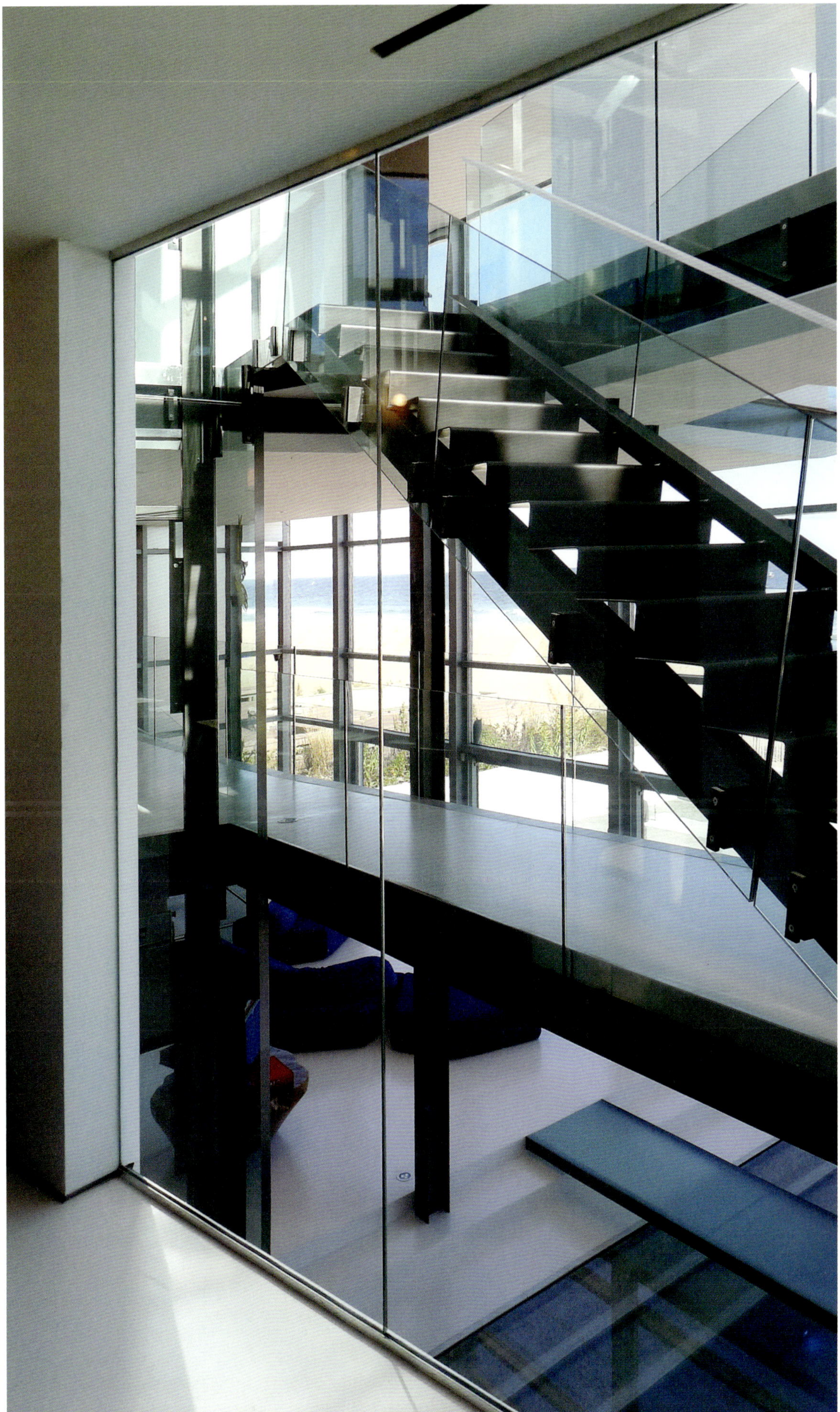

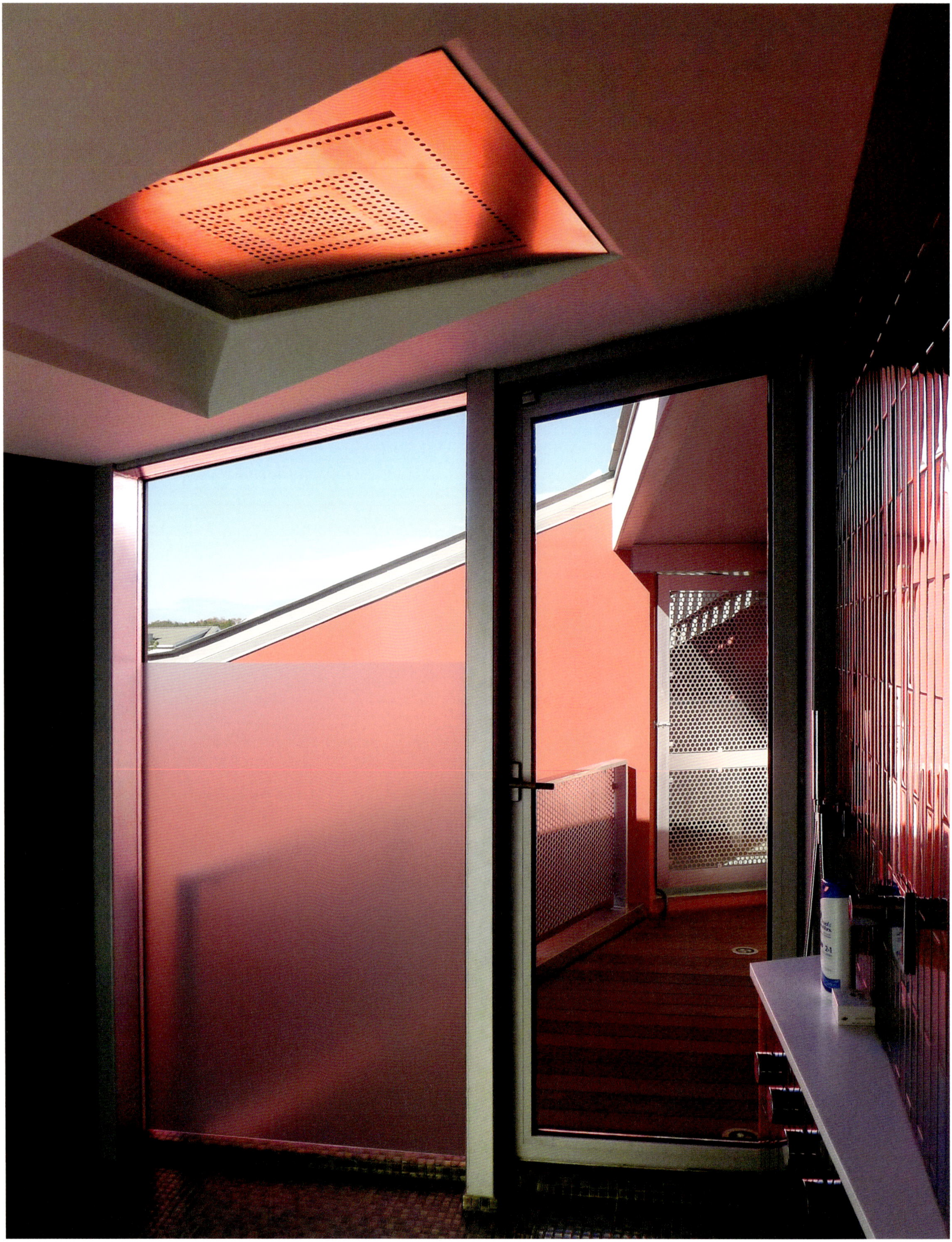

INTERVIEW

BY VLADIMIR BELOGOLOVSKY

Discovering a Small Universe in Sea Girt
Interview with David Hu
August 19, 2020

Vladimir Belogolovsky: Could you talk about how you came across architecture and decided to pursue it as a profession?

David Hu: I was born in Taipei in 1955 and grew up there in the 1960s and 70s at the time when social fabric in Taiwan was going through a lot of transition. It was the time when the American culture was pouring into Taiwan. My father was an architect, but not with his own practice. He graduated from Harbin University of Technology. Our family lived in an old single-family wooden Japanese house. When I was in my teens the city began to modernize on a large scale and many modern buildings started to come up. That's when we relocated to one of those concrete towers. That drastic shift made me very much aware of my living environment and how it was changing. That's when I realized that I was very sensitive to space and architecture in general. In fact, once we moved out, I realized how precious our original house was. It was naturally breathing, delicate, and beautiful. I have very strong and fond memories living in it. I try to keep all those memories alive in the projects that I am designing today.

VB: Since you grew up in the family of an architect you must have known a lot about architecture from your early age. And you probably traveled to see buildings, right?

DH: Actually, I grew up in a completely different era and society. There was a rule in Taiwan at the time that would restrict travel outside of the country for anyone before their military service. We used to have mandatory conscription for all males reaching the age of 18. And now Taiwan has a largely volunteer-based army. I did my military training from the age of 23 to 25. Only after that I could leave the country for the very first time. However, during my college and military service days I traveled widely around Taiwan and its smaller islands. I visited a lot of traditional and vernacular architecture.

VB: What was your experience like studying architecture first in Taiwan and then in America? What were your main lessons from some of your professors that influenced you most?

DH: First, I received my Bachelor of Science degree at the Chinese Culture University in Taipei. The education was very rigorous, and I acquired a solid knowledge, particularly in history of modern architecture. All my professors were practicing architects. Then I went to study for my Master of Architecture degree at Washington University in St. Louis. That whole experience had a very special meaning for me because everything was so new to me. I was there from 1980 to 1982. Everything I used to study from books or television, while in Taiwan, suddenly, became real. I could visit some of those buildings in the US and in other parts of the world. One of the first elective classes I took in St. Louis was History of Greek and Roman Architecture taught by a Greek Professor. Before that when I studied it in Taiwan it was quite distant to me. I couldn't touch it, so to speak. I also did very well in my design studios. There was a particular exchange with one professor who became very important. When I shared with him my work that went back several years he said, "David, you are a very good designer, but why do you repeat yourself?" [Laughs.] In a way, I was working on one kind of building. I had a lot of fascination with the work of Louis Kahn, appropriating a kind of stoic geometry. There was a sort of brutal sense to it. So, he said, "Why do you repeat yourself." At first, I was really disappointed. And then I thought, "Hey, I am still at school. What am I doing?! Am I going to emulate Kahn for the rest of my life?" I thought hard about what he said. And I realized that he was right. I think about that a lot and I try to develop insights for different projects differently. Now, I think my architecture is all over the place. [Laughs.] Well, I am not afraid of doing something for the first time. I am used to taking a risk.

VB: After graduation was there a particular reason for you to look for work in New York?

DH: I think even when I was growing up in Taiwan, I knew I would end up in New York. That was my destination. I wanted to live

David Hu

in a place where I would be continuously exposed to a rich and diverse mix of cultures, and stimulation across disciplines.

VB: But there were very few opportunities for architects in New York in the 1980s. It was not the place to be for a practicing architect. You were prepared for that kind of sacrifice, professionally, right?

DH: You are right, but I came here to follow my course and my dream. And if it had to be difficult it had to be difficult. I think having a successful career is not everything. I want to be able to enjoy my life on all levels. For example, I enjoy writing and teaching. I may not have been able to develop that if I lived elsewhere. I love living in a place where I can constantly interact with so many different people from all walks of life, from very different backgrounds. People that I can interact with make my life so much more meaningful.

VB: You worked at Philip Johnson's office, Johnson/Burgee Architects from 1985 to 1990. His work was very eclectic and different from yours, and it kept transforming over the years. What is it that you learned from that experience?

DH: That was the time when he was working on his Post-Modern projects or more precisely defined as Post-Modern Classicism. When I came to New York I wanted to work for someone who I would learn from. I wanted to focus on the profession, not a style. I learned from him every day because I worked with him very closely – one on one. It was a 70-person office, but he worked with just a handful of lead designers like me. He called us the kids. [Laughs.] Each one of us had a team – a manager, detailers, project architects, drafters. The main project I worked on was 191 Peachtree Tower finished in 1990 in Atlanta. It is a 50-story building capped by twin crowns. He famously said, "You cannot not know history." He knew some of the history books by heart. He would tell me, "David, go to such and such book, such chapter, and you will see this or that photo of a project." He was exceptionally well read and shared his knowledge all the time. He was, of course, jumping a lot and his ideas were all over the place, but for me perhaps the main lesson was this – you can't limit your imagination. And you learn from history, not only from what is happening today. History is never wrong. [Laughs.]

After Johnson's office I became a consultant. I worked for George Heery on one project in Atlanta who was familiar with 191 Peachtree Tower there and wanted to build a high-rise building with people who worked on the Tower. I was referred to him by his daughter, as we worked together at Johnson's office. So, I ended up working for him in Atlanta for about a year. Then I became very busy working in Taiwan, as it was booming then. I stayed there and formed an office GUAN HU LINTOTT with two exceptional designers, Ernest Guan and Mark Lintott, until I returned to New York in 1995 to start my own practice the next year.

VB: But wouldn't you agree that 1995-96 was not exactly a good period here in New York for architects? Why would you give up work in Taiwan and come here?

DH: Well, by then I was already convinced that Taiwan was not the place where I wanted to be, even though I was very busy there. To do good architecture you need to have a developed architectural culture. You need not just sophisticated clients, but also a professional milieu of contractors, builders, consultants, and a full range of cultural underpinnings. To be able to achieve high quality in architecture is very important. "God is in the details". It was difficult then in Taiwan or in China. And it so happened that in 1995, an acquaintance of mine, Doug Spranger, who owned a highly regarded industrial design firm here in New York asked me if I would want to start my architectural practice and work on projects together. A space for my office was available in his building. It sounded intriguing and I took that chance. I really wanted to come back to New York.

VB: This was incredibly adventurous and risky of you because New York at that time was very quiet and there was very little work even for leading architects. I was a student in the 1990s and I remember that from 1990 to 1996 there were less than a handful of big buildings built in the entire city. And none of them were even interesting. The situation was hopeless! It was only in 1999 when distinguished buildings by such architects as Christian de Portzamparc, Greg Lynn, and Bernard Tschumi were built, and the press was ecstatic calling these projects the most fantastic in a generation. That, of course, was just the beginning of what followed in the 2000s and the incredible building boom and opportunities for architects that we are still experiencing today. But at that time, you couldn't have known any of that, right?

DH: Well, you must have faith. None of that mattered. What I knew about New York was that it had the right vibes and environment. It is like a seed in a fertile soil. I read *The New York Times* on weekends, I went to the theaters, museums, galleries, lectures, I strolled the neighborhoods, and so on. All of that to me was way more important. And, I was thinking that I still could exert my influence in Asia I had to take that opportunity and I am glad I did. I was prepared for the opportunities and challenges in New York.

VB: How would you describe what you do as an architect? What would you say are the main intentions of your architecture?

DH: I believe that every time there is a major shift in architectural style it is conditioned and enabled by new technological inventions. If you go over the stylistic progression of architecture – from antiquity to modernity – you will see how new technologies make a direct effect on architectural innovation. Sure, there are many other contributing factors – social, cultural, regional, climactic, and so on. But architecture always represents a particular moment of technological de-

The Sea Girt House

velopment. So, the question is – what is our moment? For me it is about the digital age. We live in a digital time and I want to understand how it can affect architecture. How could it be used differently, designed differently, and perceived differently? Perhaps we are coming to a point when digital technology will start taking control from us, designers. So, for me architecture is not about working with styles but working with technologies. Where do we stand now as humanity? What should be the role of architecture? We need to redefine our identity as humans and architecture can help us do that. What is the difference between humanity and the AI? That's what I want to address. That's what is urgent because the time passes so quickly these days.

VB: This is fascinating to hear it from you because you graduated in the pre-digital age. The so-called digital revolution in architecture took place in early 1990s, by the way, right here at Columbia University and quickly took over the profession. Tell me – how does the digital make an effect on your work?

DH: Yes, you are right. At school we still used drafting boards. [Laughs.] But by the time I started my practice, the computers were already the essential part of practicing architecture. The Sea Girt House that we are going to talk about in more detail was all designed on computers, even though we still use sketching over tracing paper to better understand and get a feeling for the space. The computer is our partner in doing everything very precisely.

VB: Would you say that your design for the Sea Girt House was entirely conditioned by the digital tools you use? You couldn't have designed it by hand, right?

DH: Absolutely. There is no way I could have designed this project without computers. It is way too complex. Just look at the roofscape – all the different bends, an array of angles. The entire structure was manufactured in the shop. There are no two pieces there that are the same. Every piece of structure has a different angle, connections, welded parts, and so on. There is no way I could have drawn all that on paper. We no longer can draw most of our projects by hand. There are too many variants. Sure, I have my hand drawing in my mind. But the tolerance is so small, everything is so precise, there are so many different systems that pass next to each other that to be able to draw all that we need such perfect imagination of all the

8 Catherine Street, Manhattan, 2012.

locations and tolerances that it is nearly impossible to achieve without computers. We can imagine the process, but we no longer can draw that precisely.

VB: Let's go back to my earlier question – what is architecture for you?

DH: Architecture is about space that can properly represent the technologies of our time, the tectonics of our time. To me space is still the most important thing in architecture. But not just any space. It should reflect a collaborative spirit of the team – the client, architect, contractor, consultants, and so on. When I say tectonics, what I mean is that my designs are inspired by what the current technology enables me to use. For example, standing seam panel system for roofs enables me to design the Sea Girt House in a very liberating yet, in a very particular way. My design is informed by the current technologies. Tectonics explains why buildings are built certain ways throughout history. Of course, there are also codes that regulate and direct our designs.

VB: Were there any specific code restrictions for the Sea Girt House design?

DH: The house was prescribed to have a 30% slope roof because this very conservative town on the New Jersey Shore wants all houses to be alike. But my client was determined to have something different and I worked with him to achieve that. The way we were able to go around that regulation is that we covered the house with a single roof with multiple slopes and the average slope is precisely 30%. [Laughs.] And if they wanted to check that we could show them our calculations to prove it. But they did not ask us for that. They approved our design because they really liked it. So, architecture is about all of these guiding forces that become inspirations for the architect to follow. Architecture is about a truthful way of putting things together. As an architect I am willing to respond to a variety of challenges – by the code, my client's desires, site conditions, my own inspirations, and so on. And because of the new technologies, places are changing their meanings. That's what I want to capture with my architecture. I want to address the urgency of individual sense of being in space. That is something that's very important to me along with my goal for architecture to be able to transcend boundaries of styles, time, and cultural identities.

Speaking of another one of my projects, an office building at 8 Catherine Street in Chinatown in Manhattan. I did that with my partners, Suns Hung and Keitaro Nei, we called ourselves H2N. It was all about responding to the chaotic rhythm of its neighborhood. We always like to do something that's straight forward. The whole building is a straight up extrusion of its rectangular site seven times. But the structure and glass facades are spaced and subdivided in a gradated sequential way – 2 ft 3 in, 2 ft 6 in, 2 ft 9 in, 3 ft, 3 ft 3 in, and so on. There is an increased rhythm that is coming from the surrounding context. So, every glass size is different, every column has a different spacing; not random, but intentional. That's how we shape our projects – we bring together the inspirations from their place and cultural sensitivity, tectonics, and current technologies. That's how buildings become the products of their times in the most direct and honest ways. Now you walk around Chinatown you notice the building. It stands out. It is different because the times are different, the technologies are different.

VB: What did your structural engineer say when you told him about your sequencing idea?

DH: He loved it! We used the same engineer who worked on the house. He loves challenges. [Laughs.] And it did not make the building more expensive because you have to have structure anyway. The structure was not overdesigned, it was straight forward, but strategic. And it was easy to achieve different glazing panel sizes because of its frameless glazing system. So, the glass panels were simply cut to the prescribed sizes. The curtain wall system company was also the same that we used for the house. All the skylights for the house were manufactured very precisely in Shenzhen. Everything was done perfectly and shipped here to assemble, and all the pieces fit like hand and glove. It was a very fine assembly.

VB: What single-term words would you use to describe your work or the kind of architecture you want to achieve?

DH: Modern, current, technology, tectonics, spirit of place, vision of architecture's next step. Right now, the way the technology is being developed is still decided by us. But give it ten more years and we may not be in control anymore. This is a crucial time. We need to know where we want the humanity to go. If AI keeps developing so fast very soon it may not be our call anymore.

VB: Could you talk about your initial discussion with the client of the Sea Girt House and what were his objectives?

DH: He was very open. The only thing he said to me was that he wished the house would be designed as a work of art. He said, "Surprise me!" Obviously, we talked about the number and specifics such as what kind of different spaces needed to be. But that's not what was important to him. So, I had a lot of freedom. Still, we had a real site, real zoning requirements, and so on. For example, the code said that we could have two stories in the front and three stories in the back, which meant that the roof would tend to cascade towards the front. That's where the idea of a single ocean-like roof came about. The client is a writer who works from home and spends a lot of time there, wandering around like a wayfarer. He also shared with me his passion for swimming. All of these hints gave me a lot of ideas to work with.

VB: You compared the house to a landscape, painting, mental space, conceptual space, and place reflective of our time – the digital age. You also mentioned it having lungs – two central courtyards that are open to the sky and naturally ventilated. Could you describe this house for me?

DH: The client did not want any neighbors to be able to see the interior. Yet, he wanted the house to be very open and full of light. That's why most of the light comes from the top. And two courtyards are acting as lungs. And the back façade facing the ocean is also fully glazed. The inside of the house is an abstracted landscape of overlapping surfaces, columns, bridges, stairs, skylights, and shadows that dance around all day long, and all of them get reflected in a lap pool, which is very central and is seen from every vantage point in the house. The pool is crossed by a glass bridge, which is used for meditation, reflection, and contemplation, not just a crossing link. Architecture in this house finds its own essence and everyone who visits it would come across different meanings, hints, and surprises, as if exploring an abstract painting. It is a mindset, just like a traditional Chinese literati painting. There is no one narrative, no specific story. The space is not just to accommodate a family. It is all about a dialogue. The space responds to what you think.

VB: Looking at some of the drawings and photographs the space appears to be perceived as you describe it – a series of overlapped images, surfaces, spaces, and stories. You said that you designed it as "a space that opens the door for abstraction." Could you talk about how you imagined the experience of being in this collage-like house?

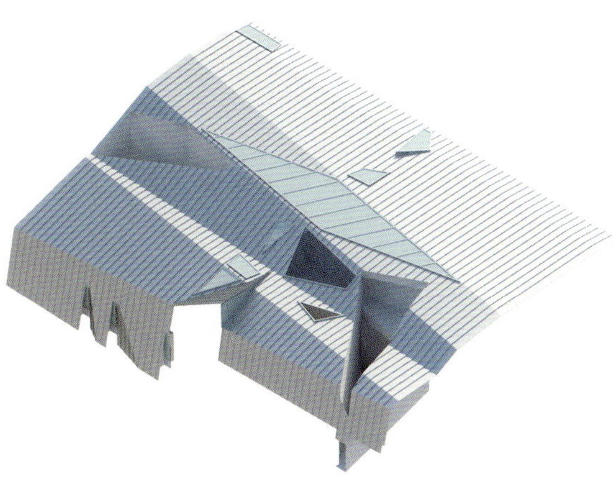

The Sea Girt House's roof

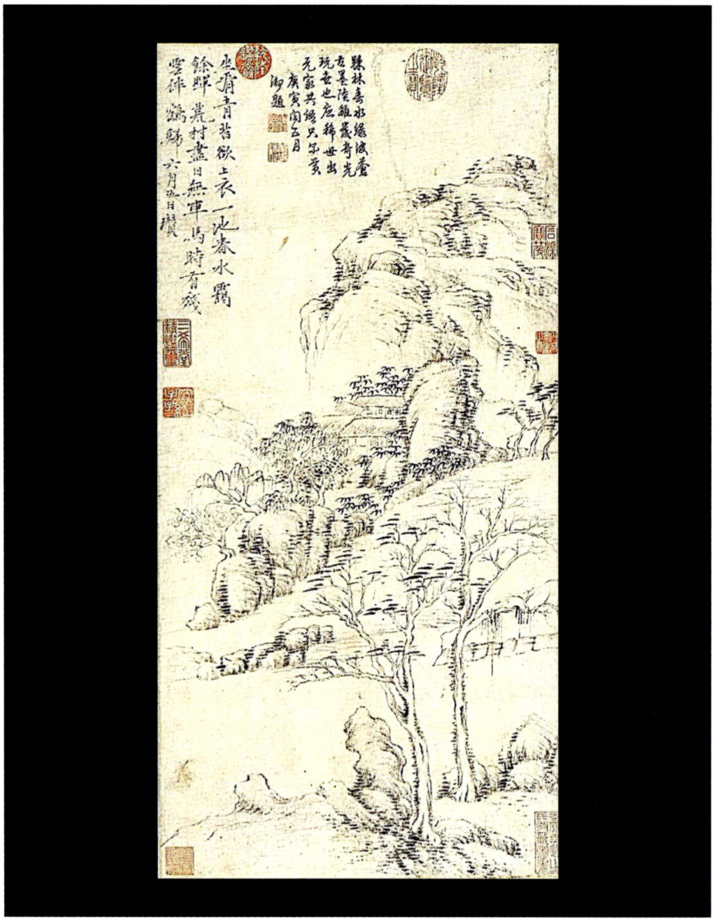

Literati painting genre began around 1100-1200 A.D.

DH: I wanted to capture a fragmentary vision that constantly gets shifted. I wanted to achieve a kind of simultaneousness of perspectives and views, not single perspective view or a panoramic view. I wanted to capture many incidents, jittering, gaps, distortions, and details that are usually left out. It is about a collage of ideas and visions. I wanted to get as close as possible to how we actually experience the world, which is never about a continuous and whole perception. That's why every floor is different, every connection from floor to floor is different. And every time you take even the same path the experience is different because it is so rich and multidimensional that you would pay attention to different things. And because the house is so open to the weather it completely transforms with it.

VB: Sounds like you are very much influenced by Deconstructivist architecture, right?

DH: Of course! But that is just one of many influences. In fact, Philip Johnson was working on the famous 1988 Deconstructivist show at MoMA during my time in the office, so I was very familiar with the work and he often reflected on it. Of course, all of the participants in the show were well published and I followed their work with great interest. They were called paper architects then, as they hardly built anything by that point. But when I design my projects, I always think about constructability every step of the way. It is not about producing cool-looking renderings. I am thinking about construction documents from the moment I start my first sketch. That's the big difference between my work and the work of those architects. I would not draw or paint something that cannot be built. How do you turn an idea into a real thing? The look and how things are made should be intrinsic.

VB: One of the strongest references for your house design is a Chinese literati painting. Could you talk about its influence on your architecture?

DH: It goes back to the tectonic idea. When I look at the Chinese paintings what's important to me is their tectonic history. I am interested in how these paintings are produced and how their quality is achieved. My enjoyment goes beyond their image and form. I enjoy the technique as well. That's what I want to achieve in my architecture. I want to express the tectonics in my work. Just like a paining is made up of different strokes my projects are assembled out of various elements. And that's what they are – just elements – columns, walls, and skylights – but when they come together, just like you feel that a painting is talking to you, I want my buildings to connect with you. That can be achieved through abstraction. For example, westerners can be moved by the Chinese paintings without understanding the meaning behind them because they feel a connection beyond meaning. Let's call this connection spiritual. A meaning is important, but to establish a connection you need to go beyond just meaning. Certain things touch us very deeply, even spiritually. And when people visit the Sea Girt House, they don't need to know how columns are made or connected, or how a skylight is manufactured and installed. But they would be amazed by the perfect shape of that skylight and how the sunlight renders and energizes the house through it.

VB: Speaking of Chinese calligraphy and painting you noted that there are eight ways that a brushstroke can be executed. How do you transfer such ideas to architecture?

DH: These principles describe how to write eight common strokes in regular script. All eight are found in one particular character 永 known as Yong or permanence. That's why these eight principles are known as *Yong zi ba fa*. Ba stands for eight. They include a tiny dash or speck, rightward stroke, downward stroke, tapering thinning curve, and so on. Practicing these brush techniques of moving your hand is meant to ensure that any beginning calligrapher would be able to achieve a beautiful handwriting. All Chinese characters are composed of just these eight basic elements. If you master them well, you can master any text, any poem. Every Chinese calligrapher follows this system. So, anyone who is familiar with it can see whether a painter is good or not. I relate these elements to building methods in architecture.

For example, there are only so many ways to support a ceiling, fix the glass, or make a bridge. In other words, there are only so many ways of building a building. In a way, these elements are like columns, beams, and arches. That's what makes up buildings. There are only so many principles behind the tectonics of architecture. Then we go to the next level – a crucial thing for achieving good quality in a painting depends on what kind of paint brush hair is used, such as goat, rabbit, or weasel. They are picked for their resilience – are they strong or soft, long or short, what kind of traction is achieved? That's why also the choice of ink and paper are important. Similarly, another level of architecture can be achieved by using various types of windows, kind of glass, and so on. All those choices will determine what kind of light will be brought into the space. That can be controlled and even finetuned on a variety of levels. That's what I mean when I say that a space can be turned into a painting. It is up to the architect's ability whether the result can be beautiful. Or take James Turrell's series of enclosed "Skyspaces" that allow to view sky through an aperture in a roof. These installations are just like paintings that transform our perception in the most beautiful ways right in front of your eyes.

VB: They inspire your work as an architect.

DH: Of course. Because they fuse paintings and architecture into one. That's very inspirational and again, spiritual. I designed a 40-story tower once in Taiwan called LJ Tower Taichung where I introduced long and narrow multistory windows with glass panes set at different angles and inlayed into the stone curtain wall system. Every piece of glass was of different size. And these panels would be grouped – one field would have one angle and another field would follow another angle. Every part of the building would look and reflect light very differently. So, every day this tower would look completely different and the perceptions from within would also be very different. The whole idea came from a hint of the client who did not want a glass building; he asked for a stone building. That's why I focused on the idea of punched windows, not a glass curtain wall. This is what concerns me most – how do I achieve uniqueness of architecture at every moment? I want to use the latest technology to achieve different affects and potentials that were not possible before. That tower was never built but imagine how special that would be! It would be like multiplying the Sea Girt House on a city scale for everyone to experience and enjoy.

VB: You said that the house is a small universe. But first, you had to fit this universe on a specific block, a row of very conservative houses facing the ocean on the New Jersey shore. Could you touch on that?

DH: Well, this is a big house and because the client did not want the interior to be seen from outside entering the house is like discovering a small universe. Once you are behind the 15-foot front door you are somewhere else. But speaking of the context what's important is that, as I already mentioned, the roof is inspired by the ocean. The way the roof is shaped reflects the

LJ Tower Taichung Taiwan tower design, 2012, (Unbuilt).

The Sea Girt House

ocean's movement. No matter where you are in the house you can look up and see the sky and the horizon.

VB: I noticed how you shifted some of the windows along the front façade. It reminds me of Daniel Libeskind's windows. He said, "A window is a window. But to me it is not about a window, it is about the idea of how you look at the world."

DH: Yes, of course. I love his work. And again, the client wanted his house to be quite private. That was the reason for manipulating the views in such ways that a passerby would not see what's inside. Yet, from within you can see the street, the sky, the ocean, and the movement of the sun and clouds.

VB: What do you think about the immediate neighboring houses; is the Sea Girt house a good neighbor?

DH: You know, from the very beginning the client said, "Don't even think about the other houses." [Laughs.] He was very honest about it. Well, they are not good looking houses. There is no character there and the client did not like them. And you know, he is the only one who lives there year-round. For everyone else these are summer houses. The argument we used in our presentations was that the houses that are lined up there along the shore are all different. There are no two houses that are done in the same style. They vary from pseudo French chateau to very eclectic and colonial models. So, we simply added yet another different house. We did not disturb any kind of existing unity.

VB: I am looking at some of the photos of this extraordinary house and I wonder – who would dare building it in such a conservative part of the country? As you know, you can drive for many miles and hours through New York, New Jersey, and some other neighboring states and not come across a single experimental house. Selecting the contractor and builder for this job must have been quite something. Could you talk about your experience of turning your drawings into a reality and what were the main challenges?

DH: We used my client's contractor friend. Of course, it was a leap of faith. And you are right, this contractor and his team never worked on such a complex and unusual house before. But when we first met, I saw people who were intrigued by the house. They were very curious to learn about it as much as possible. They had many questions and they looked forward to working on such an unusual project. There was such enthusiasm, such care. Right away they told me that they will work hard because there may not be another chance to work on another house like this in their entire careers. And what we tried to explain to them was that once the structure, which is very unusual and all custom-built in the shop, was going to be in place, it would serve as a very strong guideline basically for an assembly job – various custom elements would fall into their intended places and such standard things like metal studs and sheetrock panels would simply follow the structure. We even built a scale model and kept it on site so workmen would see what our goal was. They loved it. Anyway, there was such an incredible level of commitment on the part of the contractor and his team that I want to include all of their names in this book. I am really grateful to each and every one of them. There was such a strong comradary during this project.

VB: The house was finished in 2014. Is there anything that you would do differently today? What do you like most about this experience?

DH: Honestly, I wouldn't change a thing. And every time I talked to the client, he was very happy about the process and the result. And every time I visited the house, I liked what I saw. In fact, I love the actual house more than what the photographs capture because it is a kind of space that is very hard to document accurately with only the visual component. I am very happy about the whole experience, and it is a great house to welcome and share with people.

VB: In 2016, you were appointed as a visiting professor at the graduate architecture program at Jiao Tong University in Taiwan. Could you share that experience?

DH: This was a graduate level course for students from across different fields, not just architecture. I had literature students, for example. It was a series of history seminars, for which I would like to do a book at some point. One of the topics was to analyze a traditional Chinese literati painting. I took a break from my practice and spent a whole semester teaching. And I also learned a lot from that process because I connected with the new generation and was able to see what is it that important to them and about their concerns and interests. For that reason alone, I would like to keep in touch with academia. I like teaching from time to time. I have done this a number of times in Taiwan and here in the US at Lehigh University in Bethlehem, Pennsylvania. I also like teaching on visuality and how we interpret what we see – from history, paintings, and nature. One of my points was that you can't learn architecture from simply memorizing and copying buildings; you need to understand their intentions.

VB: What do you think about the current creative moment in architecture? Where do you think it is now and where do you think it is going?

DH: I would say we are a prolonged transition period into the digital age. We are still learning how to be comfortable with all the digital tools that are available to us. We are still trying to master them.

VB: But wouldn't you say that it is not only about technology and that there are other forces at play such as social issues, the need for architecture to serve a broader and more diverse society, address the economy of means, scarce resources, climate change, and our increasing fear of the future and fascination with the safety, comfort, and familiarity of the past?

DH: Absolutely. And what's important is that there is no longer one particular way of doing things. There are many alternatives at the same time. For example, there is a whole new movement for regional and vernacular identity search, which I see as a reaction to high tech and global models without acknowledging particularities of each place, culture, and climate. And in my own work I am open to all kinds of approaches. I am interested in exploring digital technologies, high tech, but also why not try researching more about vernacular possibilities and trying to address a regional character of a particular place? Yet, my main interest is in pushing architecture forward. And by pushing it forward I don't mean trying to find how to bend a piece of steel the way no one has done before. No, that's not what I am after. I want to discover things like – how do we improve our office environment? How do we make our living places more desirable? What alternative materials can we use to make us more comfortable? How could we make the façade systems of our typical high-rise buildings more interesting? That alone could make such a huge impact on how our cities look like.

The Sea Girt House

APPENDIX

BIOGRAPHY

David Hu was born in Taipei, Taiwan and graduated from the Chinese Culture University with a B.S. in Architecture. Upon graduation he furthered his education in the United States with a two-year Master of Architecture program at Washington University in St. Louis with a Research Assistant scholarship.

After his studies he moved to New York City and began working at the A/E firm Urbitran in 1982. During the next two years he entered numerous national and international architectural competitions. Although not awarded with any commission, nearly all of them were selected as finalists or received merit awards. One of the projects was selected by the New York Urban League for a special presentation in 1984.

He joined Philip Johnson's office in 1985 and became one of Mr. Johnson's lead design assistants. From 1990 through 1998, Mr. Hu worked as a design consultant for various architectural firms overseas and in the US including George Heery's office in Atlanta for the campus design of a global corporation. In 1999 he formed David Hu Architect to put in practice his multi-cultural sensibilities and architectural history, theory and design insights. He ensures every project will distinctively reflect the wishes of its client and articulate a unique outcome for each, and vigilantly maintain the design quality and consistency.

To further widen and deepen perspectives for architectural design, Mr. Hu lectures and teaches across the US and overseas to exchange ideas and create new dialogues. He taught design studios at Lehigh University, PA and gave multiple lectures on East, West and Converging Visual Cultures in Taipei and California. In 2016, he was appointed as a visiting professor at the graduate Architecture program at the esteemed Jiao Tong University in Taiwan. He created a curriculum and taught a semester of a visuality/design theory seminar course, "Converging Visuality of the Digital Age," developed from his lectures.

His work encompasses a variety of architecture categories and has been featured in numerous professional publications worldwide. It explores the tectonics and spatiality of architecture in the current unique visual culture to address and reflect upon our sense of Being in the Digital Age. Mr. Hu is currently working on a book that articulates the global merging of visual cultures and its impact on Humanity.

PROJECT CREDITS

Architect
David Hu Architect

Design Team
David Hu, Mark Gumienny, Javier Oddo, Sofia Dobrev, Bridgette Cruz, Derek Chen, Tamas Szalczer, Meri Takeda, Yu Chia Shi, Suyin Chia, Michael Wang.

Location
Sea Girt, New Jersey, USA

Project
Sea Girt House

Completion
2014

Built Area
11,000 SF

Photography
Wade Zimmerman, Javier Oddo, Mark Gumienny.

Structural Engineering
Mahandra Sheth

Mechanical Engineering
Plus Group Consulting Engineering. Imtiaz Mulla PIC

Construction Company
The Salmon Group. Wayne Olson PM.

Furninture and Decorationn
Moss Bureau

Curtain Wall, Skylights
Asia Building Materials, Inc. Wayne Tam PIC.

Lighting Design
Pei-Heng Tsai, Johanna Grawunder

Roofing
Capital Roofing Co. Inc.

Flooring
Decocrete

Kitchen
Boffi

Elevator
Mobility Elevator

Stairs and Railings
EeStairs America Inc

Indoor Swimming Pool
Specialized Pools

A/C and Heating Systems
Schaibles Plumbing and Heating

Electrical Systems
Yanetta Electric

Lutron Systems
Custom Electric

Fire Place
Spark Modern Fires

Security Systems
Advanced Electric

Drywall
NTS Drywall

Painting
JH Painting

Specialty Glass and Cabinetry
Fong's Creative Construction. Mr. Fong

Sound System
World Stage Inc.

PHOTOGRAPHY CAPTIONS

Birdseye view at entrance.
Photograph by Wade Zimmerman.

Cellar wall concrete form work.
Photograph by Mark Gumienny.

Cellar wall concrete form work.
Photograph by Mark Gumienny.

Cellar wall concrete form work.
Photograph by Mark Gumienny.

Cellar wall concrete form work.
Photograph by Mark Gumienny.

Cellar wall concrete form work.
Photograph by Mark Gumienny.

Cellar wall concrete form work.
Photograph by Mark Gumienny.

Cellar wall concrete form work.
Photograph by Mark Gumienny.

East curtain wall detail.
Photograph by Javier Oddo.

Cellar wall concrete form work.
Photograph by Mark Gumienny.

Cellar wall concrete form work.
Photograph by Mark Gumienny.

Cellar wall concrete form work.
Photograph by Mark Gumienny.

Cellar wall concrete form work.
Photograph by Mark Gumienny.

Cellar wall concrete form work.
Photograph by Mark Gumienny.

Cellar wall concrete form work.
Photograph by Mark Gumienny.

Cellar wall concrete form work.
Photograph by Mark Gumienny.

Cellar wall concrete form work.
Photograph by Mark Gumienny.

Steel work began.
Photograph by Mark Gumienny.

Structural steel work.
Photograph by Mark Gumienny.

Structural steel work.
Photograph by Mark Gumienny.

Structural steel work.
Photograph by Mark Gumienny.

Structural steel work.
Photograph by Mark Gumienny.

Structural steel work.
Photograph by Mark Gumienny.

Structural steel work.
Photograph by Mark Gumienny.

Steel shop.
Photograph by Mark Gumienny.

Structural steel work.
Photograph by Mark Gumienny.

Structural steel work.
Photograph by Mark Gumienny.

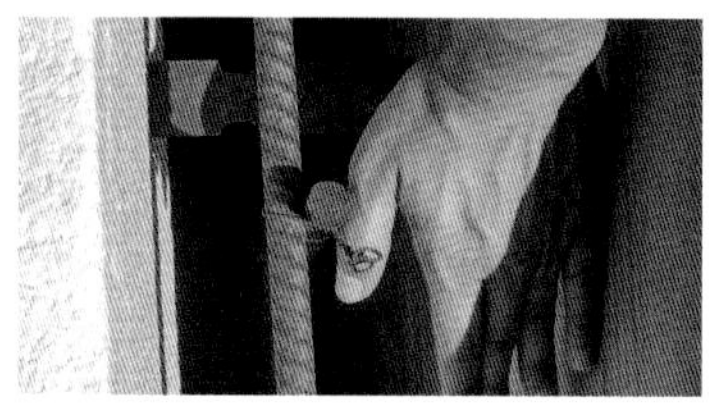
Structural steel work.
Photograph by Mark Gumienny.

Structural steel work.
Photograph by Mark Gumienny.

Structural steel work.
Photograph by Mark Gumienny.

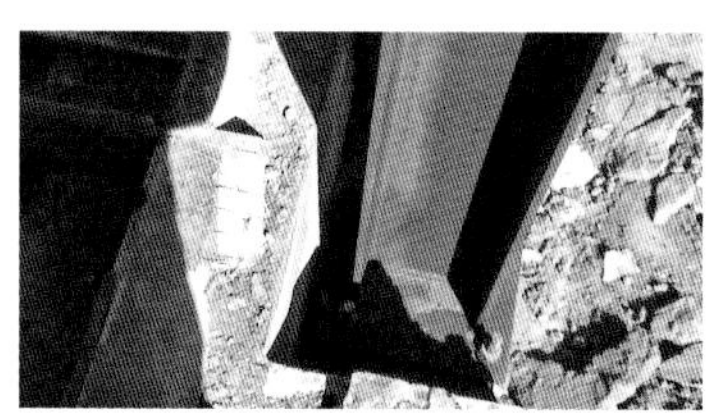
Structural steel work.
Photograph by Mark Gumienny.

Structural steel work.
Photograph by Mark Gumienny.

Structural steel work.
Photograph by Mark Gumienny.

Structural steel work.
Photograph by Mark Gumienny.

Structural steel work.
Photograph by Mark Gumienny.

Structural steel work.
Photograph by Mark Gumienny.

Structural steel work.
Photograph by Mark Gumienny.

Metal decking for roof and floors.
Photograph by Mark Gumienny.

Metal decking for roof and floors.
Photograph by Mark Gumienny.

Metal decking for roof and floors.
Photograph by Mark Gumienny.

Structural steel work.
Photograph by Mark Gumienny.

Structural steel work.
Photograph by Mark Gumienny.

Structural steel work.
Photograph by Mark Gumienny.

Structural steel work.
Photograph by Mark Gumienny.

Structural steel work.
Photograph by Mark Gumienny.

Structural steel work.
Photograph by Mark Gumienny.

Structural steel work.
Photograph by Mark Gumienny.

Structural steel work.
Photograph by Mark Gumienny.

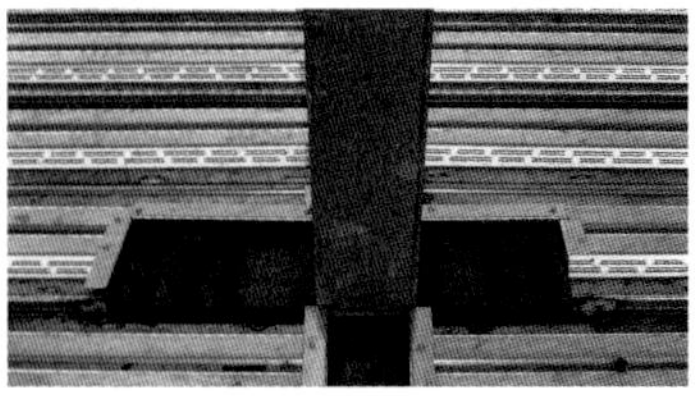

Structural steel work.
Photograph by Mark Gumienny.

Metal decking for roof and floors.
Photograph by Mark Gumienny.

Metal decking for roof and floors.
Photograph by Mark Gumienny.

Metal decking for roof and floors.
Photograph by Mark Gumienny.

Metal decking for roof and floors.
Photograph by Mark Gumienny.

Metal decking for roof and floors.
Photograph by Mark Gumienny.

Metal studs and decking.
Photograph by Mark Gumienny.

Metal studs and decking.
Photograph by Mark Gumienny.

Metal decking for roof and floors.
Photograph by Mark Gumienny.

Metal decking for roof and floors.
Photograph by Mark Gumienny.

Metal decking for roof and floors.
Photograph by Mark Gumienny.

Metal decking for roof and floors.
Photograph by Mark Gumienny.

Structural steel work.
Photograph by Mark Gumienny.

Structural steel work.
Photograph by Mark Gumienny.

Metal studs and decking.
Photograph by Mark Gumienny.

Metal studs and decking.
Photograph by Mark Gumienny.

Metal studs and decking.
Photograph by Mark Gumienny.

Metal studs and decking.
Photograph by Mark Gumienny.

Metal studs and decking.
Photograph by Mark Gumienny.

Metal studs and decking.
Photograph by Mark Gumienny.

Metal studs and decking.
Photograph by Mark Gumienny.

Metal studs and decking.
Photograph by Mark Gumienny.

Metal studs and decking.
Photograph by Mark Gumienny.

Metal studs and decking.
Photograph by Mark Gumienny.

Metal studs and decking.
Photograph by Mark Gumienny.

Metal studs and decking.
Photograph by Mark Gumienny.

Metal studs and decking.
Photograph by Mark Gumienny.

Metal studs and decking.
Photograph by Mark Gumienny.

Metal studs and decking.
Photograph by Mark Gumienny.

Metal studs and decking.
Photograph by Mark Gumienny.

Metal studs and decking.
Photograph by Mark Gumienny.

Metal studs and decking.
Photograph by Mark Gumienny.

Metal studs and decking.
Photograph by Mark Gumienny.

Metal studs and decking.
Photograph by Mark Gumienny.

Metal studs and decking.
Photograph by Mark Gumienny.

Metal studs and decking.
Photograph by Mark Gumienny.

Sheathing and waterproofing and plumbing.
Photograph by Mark Gumienny.

Sheathing and waterproofing .
Photograph by Mark Gumienny.

Metal studs and plumbing.
Photograph by Mark Gumienny.

Sheathing and waterproofing and plumbing.
Photograph by Mark Gumienny.

Sheathing and waterproofing .
Photograph by Mark Gumienny.

Sheathing and waterproofing.
Photograph by Mark Gumienny.

Roofing waterproofing.
Photograph by Mark Gumienny.

Roofing in progress.
Photograph by Mark Gumienny.

Standing seam roofing began.
Photograph by Mark Gumienny.

Standing seam roofing and waterproofing.
Photograph by Mark Gumienny.

Sheathing and waterproofing and plumbing.
Photograph by Mark Gumienny.

Sheathing and waterproofing and plumbing.
Photograph by Mark Gumienny.

Sheathing and waterproofing and plumbing.
Photograph by Mark Gumienny.

Sheathing and waterproofing and plumbing.
Photograph by Mark Gumienny.

Standing seam roof edge.
Photograph by Mark Gumienny.

Standing seam roof in progress.
Photograph by Mark Gumienny.

Bent roofing at window.
Photograph by Mark Gumienny.

View from north.
Photograph by Wade Zimmerman.

Standing seam roof outside library.
Photograph by Mark Gumienny.

Detail of standing seam roof outside library.
Photograph by Javier Oddo.

Sheathing and waterproofing and plumbing.
Photograph by Mark Gumienny.

Sheathing and plumbing.
Photograph by Mark Gumienny.

Sheathing and waterproofing and plumbing.
Photograph by Mark Gumienny.

Roofing in progress.
Photograph by Mark Gumienny.

House front view.
Photograph by Wade Zimmerman.

House front view.
Photograph by Wade Zimmerman.

Detail view north yard.
Photograph by Mark Gumienny.

View from southwest.
Photograph by Wade Zimmerman.

Roof detail at entrance.
Photograph by Wade Zimmerman.

Roof detail at south courtyard.
Photograph by Wade Zimmerman.

Roof detail at north courtyard.
Photograph by Wade Zimmerman.

Birdseye view northwest.
Photograph by Wade Zimmerman.

Door detail with side light.
Photograph by Javier Oddo.

Ocean view.
Photograph by Javier Oddo.

Library viewed from vestibule.
Photograph by Javier Oddo.

Kitchen.
Photograph by Javier Oddo.

Bending roof at windows.
Photograph by Wade Zimmerman.

Entrance stair from garage.
Photograph by Wade Zimmerman.

Bending roof at windows.
Photograph by Wade Zimmerman.

House front view.
Photograph by Wade Zimmerman.

Ocean view at entrance door.
Photograph by Javier Oddo.

Dining/Kitchen view from vestibule.
Photograph by Javier Oddo.

Pantry.
Photograph by Javier Oddo.

Dining/Kitchen viewed from library.
Photograph by Javier Oddo.

Kitchen viewed from living.
Photograph by Wade Zimmerman.

Stairs to cellar and garage.
Photograph by Mark Gumienny.

Entrance viewed from living.
Photograph by Javier Oddo.

Dining and Living rm.
Photograph by Javier Oddo.

Looking at the front door.
Photograph by Javier Oddo.

Living rm viewed from glass bridge.
Photograph by Wade Zimmerman.

Skylight viewed from Vestibule.
Photograph by Mark Gumienny.

Skylight viewed from pool.
Photograph by Javier Oddo.

Living rm viewed from Dining.
Photograph by Javier Oddo.

Entrance viewed from 1st fl bridge.
Photograph by Javier Oddo.

Pool at Vestibule.
Photograph by Wade Zimmerman.

Looking at the front door.
Photograph by Wade Zimmerman.

Living rm viewed from Dining.
Photograph by Javier Oddo.

Living rm viewed from Dining.
Photograph by Wade Zimmerman.

Looking up from entrance.
Photograph by Mark Gumienny.

Ocean view at entrance door.
Photograph by Wade Zimmerman.

Entrance skylight viewed from pool.
Photograph by Javier Oddo.

Pool looking up at 2nd
3rd floor bringes.
Photograph by Mark Gumienny.

Library viewed from grand stair.
Photograph by Wade Zimmerman.

1st fl bridge viewed
from grand stair.
Photograph by Javier Oddo.

2nd fl bridge viewed from
grand stair.
Photograph by Wade Zimmerman.

Roof detail at south courtyard.
Photograph by Wade Zimmerman.

2nd fl bridge looking south
from grand stair.
Photograph by Wade Zimmerman.

Elevator.
Photograph by Mark Gumienny.

Looking up from glass bridge.
Photograph by Mark Gumienny.

Grand stair.
Photograph by Wade Zimmerman.

Grand stair detail.
Photograph by Wade Zimmerman.

1st fl bridge viewed
from grand stair.
Photograph by Javier Oddo.

South Courtyard.
Photograph by Javier Oddo.

North Courtyard.
Photograph by Wade Zimmerman.

2nd fl bridge looking at Guest Suite.
Photograph by Wade Zimmerman.

Stairs detail.
Photograph by Wade Zimmerman.

Skylight viewed from 2nd floor.
Photograph by Javier Oddo.

Looking at the horizon from Den.
Photograph by Javier Oddo.

Guest Suite.
Photograph by Mark Gumienny.

Stairs detail.
Photograph by Mark Gumienny.

Stair from 2nd to 3rd floor.
Photograph by Wade Zimmerman.

Glass bridge viewed from 3rd floor bridge.
Photograph by Wade Zimmerman.

3rd fl bridge looking at Master BR 1.
Photograph by Wade Zimmerman.

Master BR2 door.
Photograph by Javier Oddo.

2nd fl bridge viewed from Guest Suite.
Photograph by Javier Oddo.

Stair from 2nd to 3rd floor.
Photograph by Javier Oddo.

Stair from 2nd to 3rd floor.
Photograph by Javier Oddo.

Stair from 2nd to 3rd floor.
Photograph by Wade Zimmerman.

Glass bridge viewed from 3rd floor bridge.
Photograph by Wade Zimmerman.

South Courtyard viewed from 3rd.
Photograph by Mark Gumienny.

South Courtyard viewed from 3rd.
Photograph by Wade Zimmerman.

Master BR1 door.
Photograph by Javier Oddo.

Entrance door from 3rd floor bridge.
Photograph by Wade Zimmerman.

Master BR1 door.
Photograph by Wade Zimmerman.

South Courtyard viewed from Master shower.
Photograph by Javier Oddo.

South Courtyard.
Photograph by Javier Oddo.

2nd floor shower.
Photograph by Mark Gumienny.

Master BR 1.
Photograph by Javier Oddo.

Master BR 1 bath.
Photograph by Javier Oddo.

3rd floor skylight above elevator.
Photograph by Javier Oddo.

3rd floor skylight above elevator.
Photograph by Javier Oddo.

3rd floor skylight above elevator.
Photograph by Javier Oddo.

Entrance door from 3rd floor bridge and skylight.
Photograph by Javier Oddo.

Horizon viewed from 3rd floor bridge.
Photograph by Wade Zimmerman.

Master BR 2.
Photograph by Javier Oddo.

Bathroom Master BR 2.
Photograph by Javier Oddo.

Bathroom from Master BR 2.
Photograph by Javier Oddo.

Bathroom skylight Master BR 2.
Photograph by Mark Gumienny.

Bathroom Master BR 2.
Photograph by Javier Oddo.

East yard.
Photograph by Mark Gumienny.

Master BR 2 shower-Skylight.
Photograph by Javier Oddo.

Southeast glass Corner.
Photograph by Javier Oddo.

East facade.
Photograph by Javier Oddo.

East facade.
Photograph by Wade Zimmerman.

East facade.
Photograph by Wade Zimmerman.

East facade.
Photograph by Javier Oddo.

East yard viewed from 3rd floor.
Photograph by Javier Oddo.

East facade with interior.
Photograph by Javier Oddo.

East curtain wall detail.
Photograph by Javier Oddo.

East curtain wall detail.
Photograph by Javier Oddo.

Sky and skylight.
Photograph by Javier Oddo.

East facade.
Photograph by Wade Zimmerman.

East yard viewed from 1st floor.
Photograph by Mark Gumienny.

Pool looking east at the horizon.
Photograph by Wade Zimmerman.

BOOK CREDITS

Book Layout by Julia Miceli Pitta and Lucía B. Bauzá.
Art Direction by Oscar Riera Ojeda.
Copy Editing by Michael W. Phillips Jr.

OSCAR RIERA OJEDA
PUBLISHERS

ISBN 978-1-946226-43-3
Published by Oscar Riera Ojeda Publishers Limited
Printed in China

Oscar Riera Ojeda Publishers Limited
Unit 1003-04, 10/F.,
Shanghai Industrial Investment Building,
48-62 Hennessy Road, Wanchai, Hong Kong
T: +852-3920-9300

Production Offices | China
Suit 19, Shenyun Road,
Nanshan District, Shenzhen 518055
T:+1-484-502-5400

www.oropublishers.com | www.oscarrieraojeda.com
oscar@oscarrieraojeda.com